MANDER'S
MARCH
ON ROME

*This book is dedicated to the Contadini of North
Italy and to those people in Florence, Soriano
and Rome, who, at appalling risk to their lives and
property, helped us and thousands of other escapers
in Italy in 1943 and 1944.*

MANDER'S MARCH ON ROME

d'A Mander

ALAN SUTTON
1987

ALAN SUTTON PUBLISHING
BRUNSWICK ROAD · GLOUCESTER

First published 1987

British Library Cataloguing in Publication Data

d'A Mander, *Colonel*
  Mander's march on Rome.
  1. World War, 1939–1945—Prisoners and
  prisons, Italian 2. World War, 1939–1945
  —Personal narratives, English
  3. Escapes—Italy
  I. Title
  940.5472450924   D805.I8

ISBN 0-86299-383-0

*Jacket illustration: the picture shows Battalion Headquarters of the 4th Bn
The Green Howards in the 150 Brigade Box on the Trigh Capuzzo in the
Gazala Line, the Western Desert in May/June 1942. The author is
depicted observing the advance of the Afrika Korps through his binoculars.
The picture was painted by Brigadier J.B. Oldfield OBE DL, who as
Captain Oldfield was Adjutant of the Battalion and was presumably in the
tent.*

Typesetting and origination by
Alan Sutton Publishing Limited.
Printed in Great Britain by
WBC Print Ltd Bristol.

CONTENTS

FOREWORD

This is the personal story of a regular officer in the Green Howards who, although captured in one of the toughest battles of the Desert war, refused to give up the fight. By escaping twice, his involvement with the Italian 'Resistance', gathering intelligence for the VIII Army in Italy, helping other escaped prisoners in Rome and many other activities, he helped the advancing Allied Armies in their drive for Rome in 1944; activities for which he was awarded a well deserved DSO.

I first met d'Arcy Mander in 1941 when he joined the 4th Bn The Green Howards in Weston-super-Mare as a Company Commander. I was a twenty-year-old 2nd Lt., only recently commissioned and he made a great impression on me as a thoroughly professional and dynamic soldier, qualities that stood him in good stead during the difficult and exciting times recollected in this book.

In 1941 there were four Green Howard territorial battalions in the 50th Northumbrian Division who joined the VIII Army in the Middle East and in May 1942 the 150th Infantry Brigade, comprising the 4th and 5th Green Howards and the 4th East Yorks, held a key position, the 'Box', at Got el Ualeb in Gazala, west of Tobruk. d'Arcy was now 2nd in command of the 4th Bn.

The British and German positions were some miles apart, and it was British policy to dominate this no-man's land by mobile columns known as 'Jock Columns'. Just prior to the German attack at Gazala Major General Ramsden, commanding the 50th Division, decided to send out an officer foot patrol to infiltrate enemy positions at night, lying up by day, to observe German activities for signs of imminent attack. Lt. Ewart Clay and I volunteered for this duty and it was from a 'Jock Column' commanded by d'Arcy that we set out and by happy coincidence were found, utterly exhausted, by the same column, when endeavouring to return to our own lines a few days later having completed our patrol. We owe him a debt of gratitude for being in the right place at the right time.

When the attack came the position of the 150th Brigade was vital, bearing the brunt of Rommel's main thrust against the VIII Army. In five days of hard fighting the 'Box' was surrounded, the Brigade's ammunition exhausted and the position finally overrun on 1st June. Perhaps Field Marshal Rommel should be allowed to sum up the battle, as quoted by Brigadier Young in his book *Rommel*.

'The British defence was conducted with considerable skill. As usual the British fought to the last round of ammunition.'

This is therefore the starting point of d'Arcy's personal story. I was lucky enough not to be captured so I did not meet him again until after the war. However I think we were very close to each other on 5 June 1944 when I with two other Green Howard officers entered Rome 'unofficially'. We were from the 1st Bn which had been in the Anzio beachhead until the break-out and advance to the Tiber. We were duly reprimanded by the Commanding Officer, as Rome was an American preserve.

The 1st Bn in the 5th Infantry Division had reached Anzio via the invasion of Sicily and Italy, taking part in heavy fighting on both the east and west sides of Italy before going into the Anzio beachhead where I joined them as a Company Commander. After the breakout we moved up the coast, stopping just short of Ostia and it was from there that we started out on our little adventure to represent the Regiment at the capture of Rome.

It has given me great pleasure to be invited to write a foreword to this book, which enables me to pay tribute to a friend whose qualities as a man and a soldier I have known and respected for over 40 years.

Peter Howell

PREFACE

A critical reviewer wrote something along the following lines:

'The story goes on and on, adventurous incident piled on incident until interest fades. Besides, what do they amount to, these hair's breadth escapes, narrow shaves and the rest? Buchan invented better ones. Truth is less readable than fiction and the story is as stale as yesterday's newspaper. One is becoming bored by these stories as by their tellers, beamish boys galumphing their way home through a tangle of generous peasants, Fascist spies and boastful partisans. Cave life in the mountains, chianti and pasta asciutta in lofts by candlelight, tappings on the shutter, sudden arrivals and hasty departures . . . all are now situational clichés unredeemed as a rule by literary skill.'

This cruel critique, which unfortunately fits my story like a glove, caused me to put off writing an account of my time as an escaped prisoner for over 20 years. There were no 'tappings on the shutter' but everything else is there. I must warn you also that I cannot lay claim to any literary skill.

What then can I say to justify producing yet another tale of this sort? Firstly, it is true, it actually happened, and secondly, I think the generosity and the bravery of the 'generous peasants' is worthy of mention and should be recorded. They cannot be praised too highly, and since I and many other 'galumphing beamish boys' owe more than we can ever repay to them, I have dedicated this book to all those Italians who fed us, accommodated us and helped us in every possible way at enormous risk to their lives and property.

I would also like to pay tribute to the thousands of POWs, many of whom were transported to Germany with no chance of escape, others who took their chance and were recaptured, and also those who managed very much better than I and got through enemy lines much more quickly and have never bothered or thought it worthwhile to write a book about it. Lt. Col. MacDonnell DSO, 7th Bn The Green Howards was one of these; he marched down the coast, got into a fishing boat and sailed without any fuss or bother back to our own lines and he has never ceased to urge me to put my story on paper. If I had had any sense I too would have gone down to the coast and done just that. Another was my Batman in Campo 29, who got on a train to

Naples and then went by bicycle straight through to the VIII Army. He got back to England and wrote to my wife to tell her I was well when he escaped only about four or five weeks previously. It took me ten months!

In Chapter 1, I have drawn on an account of the part played by the 150th Infantry Brigade T.A. in the Gazala Battle of 1942. This account was written by Lt. Col. W.E. Bush DSO MC, the Officer Commanding the 5th Bn The Green Howards in Campo 29, with the assistance of the Commanding Officers of all the major units of 150 Brigade; Major Dobson the Brigade Major and most of the surviving senior officers, myself included, who were all incarcerated in the Camp. It was written whilst still fresh in our minds, and we were able to compare notes with other officers who had taken part in the battles round our position and had also been taken prisoner. One of these was Lt. Col. Foote DSO, who was awarded the VC for his part in the fighting just north of our position before being taken prisoner. The original document was seized by the Italians during a search following an escape from the camp but it was immediately re-written. This copy was lost when Lt. Col. Bush escaped and was on the run for several months in the mountains of North Italy. However, it was re-written yet again in Switzerland where he and a number of other survivors, including four of the Commanding Officers, the Brigade Major and seven other officers of 150 Brigade, stayed until the Allies reached the borders of Switzerland in 1944–5.

All the characters in this book are real people and, with one exception, the names used are their proper names and the ranks given are those they held during that time. The one exception is Daniele, who is an actual person but this was not his real name. He was in a great deal of trouble when I left Rome and I do not want to re-open old wounds, which may by now be healed and forgotten.

I would also like to thank Colonel Geoffrey Powell, MC of The Green Howards and Kenneth Rankin of Odiham and Mr Alasdair White of the Deva Book Shop in Hartley Wintney for their advice and assistance in getting this book published. I am also most grateful to my old firm, Sir Owen Williams and Partners, for their encouragement and assistance in producing the maps and to my daughter Judy for her help with the typing.

Finally I would like to say a very big 'Thank you' to Brigadier J.B. Oldfield OBE DL, who produced the beautiful picture on the cover of the 4th Bn The Green Howards Headquarters on the Trigh Capuzzo.

As Captain and Adjutant of the 4th Bn, John was there in 1942 and he and I were captured at the same time. After a time in a Prison Camp in Italy he was taken to Germany where he remained until liberated by the Allies in 1945.

d'A Mander
1987

150 BRIGADE

'Here we bloody are and here we bloody stay.
Nolens bloody volens.'

In May 1942 our front line in the Western Desert, which rested on the Mediterranean at Ain Gazala, some 40 miles to the west of Tobruk, curved gently back to Bir Hacheim, approximately 45 miles south west of Tobruk. The 1st South African Division plus one Brigade were on the coast, then came 69th and 151st Brigades of the 50th Northumbrian Division T.A. To the south was a gap of 6 miles and then came the 150th Brigade, also of the 50th Division, astride the Trigh Capuzzo and the Trigh el Abd, holding a front of about 3 miles. To the south of the 150th Brigade, was another gap of some 12 miles to Bir Hacheim, where the Free French were the defenders. The whole front was covered by minefields and these were protected by constant patrolling which kept the enemy at bay and dominated the no-man's land between the two armies.

The composition of these patrols into no-man's land varied from 'Jock Columns' consisting of a company of infantry, a battery of field artillery with perhaps anti-tank and anti-aircraft guns, carriers and machine guns to small infantry night patrols of 2 to 6 men. The South Africans used armoured cars by day and these were out in front of their line on the 2 May 1942. On the 50th Division front I was in command of a 'Jock Column' consisting of one company of the 4th Bn The Green Howards and one battery of the 72nd Field Regiment, under the command of the very experienced Major Elliot, which was making its presence felt. We took with us an Officer's patrol in the shape of Lts. Ewart Clay and Peter Howell, both volunteers from the 4th Green Howards. We had to launch them into the desert and their duty was to penetrate the enemy lines by night, lie up and observe during the day and to give warning of enemy attack. Luckily we found them at the end of their ordeal and were able to bring them safely back with us to 150 Brigade when we came in.

We set out on 22nd May and had a lively time harrassing the enemy and probing his positions. The situation was tense, we knew that the Germans had built up their strength and we were in daily expectation of an attack or a possible strike by our forces against the German lines of communication.

From the 22nd to the 25th the Germans had responded to our every move in a most 'lively' fashion and our guns had fired some 50–70 rounds per gun every day. We were due to hand over to another 'Jock Column' from 69th Brigade on the 26th and that morning the enemy were strangely quiet. At 2.30 p.m. we stopped firing and were preparing to move quietly back to base when suddenly the desert erupted into life and it seemed to us that the entire Afrika Korps were advancing towards us under the cover of artillery fire. We withdrew fairly smartly but in good order, each troop of guns leap-frogging its way back and thus providing continuous support for the column as we were chased back to our minefield. However, as they came into range of the field and medium artillery of the main 50th Division positions the enemy attack was not pressed home although an air strike by six Stukas of the Luftwaffe was indeed pressed warmly home as we filtered our way back through the minefield.

Rommel's great advance, which led to the capture of Tobruk and Mersa Matruh and was only stemmed at el Alamein, had begun.

The German method of attack was to advance in great strength over a wide front under cover of artillery fire seeking the gaps in our positions and trying to penetrate where little or no resistance was met, but they checked and held off where they met determined resistance and fell back under counter-attack.

Back at 150 Brigade we quickly learnt that the enemy had executed a wide turning movement and had driven the Free French out of Bir Hacheim to our left rear and had then closed up to the rear of our position. Shortly after this they got through the minefield in the gap to the north of us and we came under attack from the right flank and thus were completely surrounded.

I was the 2nd in command of the 4th Bn; our Commanding Officer was Lt. Col. L.C. Cooper, a sheep farmer from Western Australia, who had only recently arrived. He was very active in sending out patrols and mounting counter-attacks and as a kind of spare file I was kept pretty busy. Indeed I had hardly got back from my 'Jock Column' before he sent me with a 3in. mortar team right through the minefield to see what was going on the far side and stir things up a bit. When we arrived we shot up a large concentration of vehicles, drawing

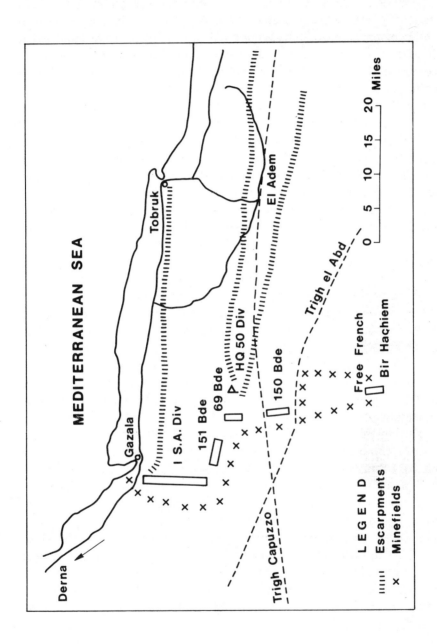

down upon ourselves an avalanche of artillery and machine gun fire. I remember directing operations from a ridge and seeing a bit of wire right under my nose, which under investigation proved to be one of our own anti-personnel mines. If I had gone another yard I would have detonated it. It went off anyway when a large shell exploded in front of me and I commenced my withdrawal airborne by the force of the explosion! We all managed to get back, although I recall having to carry the 3in. mortar barrel all the way back as we had one or two wounded in our little battle.

The story of the next few days of fighting, with ever decreasing forces and ammunition, has been told by Lt. Col. Bush DSO MC in his booklet, *150th Infantry Brigade (50th Northumbrian Division) in the Middle East June '41 to June '42*. The skirmishes, the attacks, counter attacks, the patrols, the men pinned in their slit trenches in the heat of the day with dwindling supplies of ammunition, food and water and the numerous rapid and complex moves of units and sub-units would take up too much space in this book, but mention must be made of the toughness, tenacity, endurance and bravery of those civilian soldiers of our Territorial Army. The Afrika Korps paid us the compliment of holding off when their massive waves hit our defences. They might get through minefields, but we drove them out when they did so. Unfortunately, at the rear of the Brigade position, where the field ambulance, the Sappers and Brigade H.Q. were situated, our defences were of necessity thin and scattered, and the enemy were able to penetrate our position and surround and capture the field ambulance and the Sappers. They also compelled Brigade H.Q. and the Gunners to move into the front line areas.

During this period, when we were completely surrounded and cut off, we captured one or two prisoners and also lost some of our own chaps. I remember Lt. Booth MC being sent out with a fighting patrol and failing to make the rendezvous in the morning. If the prisoner was German I was generally sent for in order to carry out a preliminary interrogation and establish the identity of the unit we had opposite to us. On one occasion our battalion shot down a Fiesler Storch aircraft, which wobbled into the ground in the minefield and we sent out a party to investigate. They found that the pilot had been killed and brought in the passenger covered in the pilot's blood. He was brought to me in a dug-out at Battalion Headquarters and the interrogation went something like this.

Me, in German.

'Sit down, Paybook!'

(All German soldiers carry their pay book (a mine of information) on them at all times).

Reading from his pay book I continued:

'So you are an officer eh?'

'2nd Lieutenant!'

'Lieutenant!'

'Captain!'

'Major!'

'Lt. Colonel!'

(From now on in a rather less ferocious tone of voice.)

'Colonel!'

'Major General!!'

'Lt. General!!!'

'I am so sorry I spoke so roughly to you General Cruewel. I had no idea who you were. Are you alright? Can we clean you up a bit? Is there anything I can do for you?'

Lt. General Cruewel was the commander of Rommel's Afrika Korps and was quite a prize. He told me he would be alright if he could have a wash and said there was something I could do for him. He informed me that he was wearing the 'Pour La Merité', the German equivalent of the VC when he was captured, that one of our chaps had taken it and he would very much like to have it back. A few words with the Sergeant in charge of the party produced the decoration, which I handed to the General. He was then consigned to the care and hospitality of Brigadier Haydon, our Brigade Commander, who arranged for his onward journey to G.H.Q. in a tank that night.

From the 29th to 31st May six major attacks were launched against us and all but two, which came from the rear, were beaten off. 232 Field Company R.E. were captured on the 30th May and on the 31st another attack penetrated between B and C Companies of the 4th Bn The East Yorkshire Regiment who were defending the rear and reached the very centre of our position immediately behind the 4th Green Howards. Captain Paul Watson commanding C Company 4th Green Howards had repelled an attack on the Trigh Capuzzo Gap on 29th May, driven the enemy back through the minefield and was wounded when he personally replaced the mines which had been lifted by the enemy. He was awarded the DSO for his bravery in this action. Immediately to the rear of C Company, Major Brian Jackson commanding B Company repelled another attack on the 31st May. He was severely wounded and later died as a prisoner in German hands. As

2nd in command of the Battalion early on 1st June I was sent to take command of the B Company sector.

At about 9 o'clock that morning Brigadier Bill Haydon was killed. He was a fighting soldier of the old school who led from the front. The last words I heard from him after I got back with my 'Jock Column' were:

> 'Here we bloody are and
> Here we bloody stay,
> Nolens bloody volens.'

He had commanded the Brigade in France and Belgium in 1939/40 and had earned the respect and awe of every man in the Brigade.

With shot and shell flying about from almost every point of the compass I made my way on foot to B Company H.Q. I found the Company Sergeant Major in a state of collapse and, before setting out to visit the platoons in my command, I laid my revolver, field glasses and a box of grenades in the Company Command Post. Guided by an orderly, I set out to look round Company H.Q. Hardly had I commenced this task before we were attacked from the rear by the usual full panoply of Germans with infantry on foot escorting various fighting vehicles, one of which was a 4-barrelled anti-aircraft cannon, probably 20 mm calibre.

I shouted to the orderly: 'Down!'

We both dived into slit trenches, I cursing because I had no weapon, when my orderly called out:

'Shall I fire sir?'

But the answer came from the Germans as the barrels of the Pom Pom were depressed and we were treated to a fusillade of explosive cannon shells and a hail of stones and splinters rained down on us.

Having arrived only minutes earlier I dived under some rubbish and heard the Germans calling:

'Come out Major Mander.'

'Come out Major Mander.'

I was soon discovered and ignominiously hauled out. Company H.Q. and the three platoons, which were spread out over a front of 2000–3000 yards; and which I had not even had time to visit, were winkled out one after another.

At the time of our capture food, water and ammunition in the 150 Brigade 'Box' were pretty low and the men had suffered from being pinned in their slit trenches through the heat of the day on very short rations. I shouted to them to collect and take with them all the water and food they could lay their hands on but was roughly silenced by a German officer who indicated forcefully that he was the one giving the orders and that I could shut up or I would be shot. I shut up!

After much confusion, dust and noise we were herded along after dark we knew not where. It seemed sensible to take stock of our position. We had wounded with us, only the most serious of whom the Germans took away for emergency operations or treatment. As the senior officer present, I collected all the food and water together and 'sat on it', giving a small ration only to the wounded. I remember telling someone to open a tin of pineapple, to give to the wounded, which we got open with great difficulty, but in the process a hole had been made in the bottom of the tin and the precious juice had trickled out on to the sand.

That night we were bundled into trucks and bumped, lurched and swayed over the desert throughout the night and the next day our Italian drivers didn't seem to know where they were. It was at that time that I began to learn Italian, starting with the words pane (bread) and aqua (water) of which we were in great need. However that afternoon we were bowling along a road in the cultivated part of Cyrenaica which none of us had ever seen before and eventually arrived in Derna, where we were sadly reunited with many of our comrades from other Battalions of the Brigade whom we had hoped might have escaped to fight another day. At Derna we were given thin straw mats on bare stone floors to sleep on, no hardship as none of us had slept in a bed for some considerable time. The latrines, however, were another matter being ankle deep in filth with only our hands to clean them out.

From Derna we were taken to a camp near Benghazi where an incident occurred which might have taken a very ugly turn. Apparently the Italians had captured an order which laid down that British soldiers must not fraternise with, i.e. give cigarettes and tea to their prisoners before taking them to be interrogated. Mussolini chose to interpret this as an order that Italian prisoners were to be deprived of food and drink and thus softened up by ill-treatment before interrogation. Incidentally none of us was ever interrogated. He therefore gave orders that no food or drink was to be given to any Allied prisoners until this order had been withdrawn. The first we knew of this situation was that the sentries were doubled and seemed to be very nervous. Machine guns were brought out and positioned to cover our compound and we were then given the news. The Senior British Officer ordered me to take charge of all the food and water and I found myself 'sitting on it' again for the second time in three days.

Earlier that day I had been involved in an unpleasant incident. With another officer I was shaking out our blankets and was about to hang them on the wire to air, when the Italian sentry, who had probably told me not to do it, upped with his rifle and shot me through my trousers and I received some slight punctures in the legs. I hurled down the blanket and marched off white with fury demanding to see the Commandante who explained the rules about blankets on the barbed wire. No great harm was done except to my trousers and that evening the 'no food, no water' order was rescinded. A bumper meal of Italian bully beef stew was issued to mark the occasion.

We now heard that we were to be flown to Italy and my thoughts turned immediately to the subject of escape. The best time to get away is, of course, straight after capture, and even I, with no experience of later difficulties, could see a number of golden opportunities during the first hours of captivity. But we had wounded with us and I was the senior officer of my little group, so although there were were many occasions when I could have dropped quietly off the truck, I felt it to be my duty to care for those who were quite seriously wounded and try to make their journey over the desert in the back of an Italian lorry as easy as possible – thus losing my first opportunity of escape.

This flight to Italy therefore presented the first practical chance of escape. My plan was simplicity itself; we would surprise and over-power the guards, then using their weapons take over the aircraft. We had an RAF pilot with us, whom we dressed as an infantryman in case they took special precautions with him; he was to fly us at ground or sea level eastwards towards the VIII Army. But we had some senior officers with us and it was necessary to get their permission for the plan and they didn't like the idea. The senior officer whose approval I had to obtain was a rather elderly Lt. Colonel, who took the view that he had done his bit and that for him the war was over. He didn't see why he should be pressured into some lunatic scheme by a young puppy he didn't know and who wanted to break his neck in some sort of suicide attempt at escape. I don't think he gave the idea any thought, he just dismissed it. He didn't actually say 'No', just agreeing to give the signal if he thought there was a good chance of success, but in his heart of hearts he had no intention of permitting us to go into action. We were driven under escort to an airport near Benghazi and loaded onto a three-engined Italian Savoia Transport aircraft. I recall the very smart, highly-scented Italian Air Force pilot with exiguous blue shirt and shorts, who wore his badges of rank in miniature on the legs of his shorts! There was a tough-looking Sergente who manned the sponson-mounted machine gun turrets towards the back of the aircraft and there were two armed Italian sentries in the middle.

I placed myself alongside one of the sentries and the other three who were in the scheme positioned themselves similarly alongside sentries. At a signal we could have knocked out the guards, seized their rifles and held up the air gunner, whose main armament pointed outside the aircraft but who also carried a pistol. With two rifles and a pistol we could have hijacked the aircraft and flown it, at ground level as far eastwards as fuel would allow, landed it and started walking towards our own lines. When you think of the ease with which hijackers operate today it seems incredible that our Senior Officer should have hesitated. We waited for him to remove his white neck scarf, the signal to proceed, throughout the flight but it remained firmly in place and we could only fume silently in our seats all the way across the Mediterranean to Bari.

From the airport we were taken to Lecce where we were marched to an old tobacco factory which was called a 'Disinfestation Station'. Needless to say we had picked up every Middle-Eastern–Mediterranean bug from our bedding and it was not uncommon for anyone to have a matchbox full of corpses in the morning. A day or two later we were de-loused in hot showers and moved to a new compound but were told to bring our mattresses with us so, of course, we brought our bugs with us to our new quarters in the old mattresses.

After a day or two, with the fall of Tobruk and the arrival of many South African prisoners we were moved by train at night up the east coast of Italy to the Po Valley coming to a halt at Piacenza on the main line to Milan. Here we were shunted on to a side-line and arrived at the Station of Ponte del Olio in the middle of the afternoon.

On our arrival we were taken to a nice little waiting room and our guards produced a glass of very pleasant white wine as a gesture of welcome. I recall that I, boorishly, remembering that these people were our enemies, refused to drink their damned wine, but was roundly told to drink up and be a good boy.

Following this welcome we were marched a mile or two up the side of the valley to a monastery which had been surrounded with a triple fence of barbed wire – there was even wire all over the roof – and converted into a Prison Camp, Campo di Concentramento No. 29.

   On arrival we were taken to a wooden hut at the back of the building where we were strip-searched and any clothing or objects which might aid escape were removed and put in a sequestration store in the guards' quarters. Luckily I had taken to keeping my watch and signet ring in my socks and when searched they remained hidden and I was able to put the socks on again with my only precious possessions safely inside. This had proved to be an excellent way of defeating searches and looters but it did make marching any distance quite a painful experience. We were then marched into the camp where we were welcomed most warmly by the Senior British Officers' staff formed from older lags who ran the interior economy of the camp.

II

CAMPO 29

Although we did not appreciate it at the time, we were lucky to find ourselves in Campo di Concentramento No. 29. It was a substantial brick building, which had been converted into a monastery or a college for novices prior to being requisitioned as a prison camp. The older part of the building consisted of two wings. To the south was what had been the Abbot's quarters and a chapel. The rest of the old building was, by the time we got there, a large refectory with cells above. At a later date, probably not long before the war, a north wing had been added, obviously for the accommodation of novices. This consisted mainly of cells and dormitories in which we were accommodated.

The rooms were clean, new and bare, iron bedsteads, mattresses, sheets and blankets were provided; there was even a cupboard for our non-existent clothes and belongings. The more senior officers (Brigadiers, Colonels and Lt. Colonels) occupied the rather larger rooms over the refectory and we; Majors, Captains etc took up residence in the north wing. I shared a cell with Major Dennis Whitehead MC TD, of the 5th Bn The Green Howards, a Territorial who was an Estate Agent in civilian life. We shared that cell for 14 months and I can tell you that at times it seemed to us more like 14 years. Also in the Camp with us were a number of British soldiers who acted as cooks and orderlies and, running the whole show was the Senior British Officer, Colonel Younghusband and his staff of British officers, all of course prisoners like us. And very well they ran it too.

The Camp lay in the foothills of the Apennines to the south of Piacenza overlooking the Po valley to the north. The Commandante was an elderly Italian Cavalry officer and a gentleman. He tried to treat us as well as he was able, but the Senior British Officer (SBO) and his staff must take the credit for the excellent way in which the camp was so smoothly and efficiently run.

Behind the Camp our Italian guards were accommodated in a wired-in compound, and I may say they did the job of guarding us very efficiently. Of the many who escaped from camps all over Italy I do not think that a single prisoner succeeded in getting out of the country until the fall of Mussolini and the advent of the Badoglio government in 1943, which made it all much easier.

Our camp was designated a 'Senior Officers Camp' and since a senior Italian officer was probably an elderly gent long past active campaigning and sleeping in ditches, we were possibly pampered just a little bit more than those who found themselves in the general run of these establishments.

As I said earlier, we were lucky to be in Campo 29 and although we had plenty to complain about we were certainly a good deal better off than those interned in other camps I have since read about. These mostly consisted of wooden huts with bunks to sleep in and no other room in which to sit, talk, eat or play cards. So far as I can gather cooking was done individually or on a hut basis with no centrally organised cookhouse with rations divided out among the inmates. The meals and general conditions must therefore have been far worse than those we had to endure.

From June 1942 until September 1943 I was a prisoner of war in this camp, and during this period we lived a 'cow-in-a-field' sort of existence. That 14 months covers the longest and also the dullest part of this story. Like the desert we had left it was monotonous and featureless, but a description of our existence there might be of interest to those who haven't experienced being in gaol.

In some ways it was like school. For instance there were lessons and lectures on a wide variety of subjects but they were voluntary. The food was awful and inadequate. The lack of privacy, the routine, the sameness of each week made it in some respects a little like a Dickensian boarding school. There we had been sent and there we stayed, like it or not. Of course there were many differences, we were a long way from home and although we did receive Red Cross parcels and letters from home at irregular intervals, the geographical distance, which was about 600–800 miles, was no measure of our feeling of isolation from our families, our homes and our own people. We might as well have been on the South Pole without a boat.

The Italians were very good at keeping prisoners of war captive, much better than the Germans. Campo 29 was very difficult to run away from and although there were some brave, some hilarious and some ingenious escapes, which resulted in one or more getting clean away, nobody from our camp ever got out of the country. Until the Armistice of 1943, I never heard of anyone ever getting to Switzerland where they would have been promptly interned, and from whence it was even more difficult to escape.

When I joined the camp as a new boy in the summer term of 1942, so far as I remember, I had a pair of khaki drill trousers with two bullet holes through each leg and a thin khaki shirt. These together with a pair of socks, a pair of pants and a pair of desert boots comprised my worldly possessions. My desert boots were lovely rough untanned leather boots with thick rubber soles and were most comfortable. Mine gave me some pain while walking because I had my wristwatch hidden in one and my signet ring in the other. Both these items survived all searches, strippings, disinfestations etc and my ring I am wearing today.

I have mentioned the Commandante and I think the Capitano, the Interpreter, was also a decent chap, but there was always a Fascist in the camp whose main function was to see that we were not treated any better than was absolutely necessary and to make sure that the guards didn't get too friendly with the guarded.

Until one has actually been put inside a prison you do not appreciate how extremely difficult it is to get out. If we had only known how almost every loophole was going to be closed tight, I am sure we would all have shown a great deal more initiative in making a break for it on the journey to the camp. Any old lag would have seen his chance and been off in a flash, but we new boys were led like lambs to the slaughter. Later, with the experience of some 14 months behind wire, and having seen numerous attempts to escape, I was very much quicker in recognizing any opportunity that offered itself and seizing it immediately and, strangely enough, being successful on a number of occasions.

The highest marks at our 'school' were given to those who succeeded in escaping. A mass breakout would merit top marks and a solo effort would be a close second. Alas I never got onto the prize list, although I was of some assistance to one or two with more imagination than I. I could see no way out of the confounded place except one which unfortunately the senior officers didn't think was a good idea.

My plan was simple: our exercise yard was bounded by a high brick wall on three sides. One could see the sentries on the outside from the upper storey windows. I proposed that a large number of us (there were nearly 200 of us) should push the wall over – with rhythmic shoving I reckoned it could be done in seconds and those who wished to leave could scramble over the wire and dash into the vineyard, over the fields, into the woods and away, while the rest could make suitable diversionary noises or even pick some grapes if they liked. The trouble was that one or more of the sentries might get hurt or even killed if the wall fell on them and some of us would quite likely get shot as the Italians were excitable and opened fire at the slightest chance, sometimes for no reason at all, as the holes in my trousers well testified. Finally, of course, we should lose our exercise yard.

The reader may wonder why I didn't get on with the idea, gather a few like-minded chaps, push the wall over and run for it, possibly with a few more holes in my trousers, even at the risk of flattening one or more of the enemy which might of course have made life unpleasant for those who remained behind in the camp. But the rules forbade it. You had to report any ideas you might have for absconding to one of the senior officers, who if they liked the idea would see to it that the resources of the camp were put behind the scheme and that no other activity or attempt would be allowed which might harm or hinder it and who, if he didn't like the idea, would simply forbid it. The system worked very well and I was able to help one or two who successfully got away by doing a little forgery, tailoring and model-making (a dummy head for leaving in the bed) to relieve the tedium of what was inevitably a very dull existence.

I have mentioned the exercise yard which lay to the north side of the camp under the windows of the New Wing and whose walls I wanted to flatten like Joshua at Jericho. But there was another smaller yard, more of a quadrangle, surrounded on three sides by the Italian Wing, the Refectory and the south aspect of the New Wing. The front of this yard, which gave onto a pleasant garden was wired in by a double wire fence constantly patrolled by Italian sentries. In this yard most of the business of the camp was conducted. The Camp shop opened onto it. Those who wanted to read sat in the sun leaning up against the wall. The buying and selling of Red Cross items was conducted here and if you wanted to bet on any mortal thing under the sun Major Fieldhouse, a chartered accountant and the Camp Bookie, would lay you odds on it. I recall the betting on the fate of the pretty young woman who walked around the camp from time to time, the daughter of the farmer next door and who would be the most likely to . . . and so on. The corner of the yard in which this group assembled was always the most lively in the camp and to listen to their cheerful conversation would take one out of our wired-in world in a way that never ceased to amaze me.

There were some who just took it all in their stride. Like me they could not see any way out of the place and so they settled down to pass the time as congenially as they could. I suppose we all did so, but I found acceptance impossible. Such a way of life was so uneventful and dull that although it had its moments: its quarrels, its ups and downs, each magnified out of all proportion because being compressed together we lived a sort of test-tube existence. It wasn't very interesting or exciting and would be dusty material for a book. Some there were who just gave up and merely 'existed' – they thought perhaps that they could continue like this indefinitely and that they would come out of it all much as you would wake after a long sleep. But you don't. You either progress or you go backwards in this life and those who did nothing, got out of the way of shaving etc, simply went downhill and you could almost see them going.

Another aspect of our existence that had an insidious and very lowering effect on our morale was the lack of any time limit. There was no sentence at the end of which you would be released. When we were captured the German Afrika Korps rolled powerfully on to the gates of Alexandria. The German Armies in Russia were penetrating deep into the Caucasus, were attacking Stalingrad and knocking at the gates of Moscow. The Japanese, who had overrun South East Asia and captured Singapore were now advancing across Burma and would soon reach the frontiers of India. It looked as though there was little to stop the Germans from the West meeting the Japanese from the East in the middle of India.

The term of our captivity seemed endless, and our hopes of seeing our homes and families again seemed to recede even as the battle receded to the east. It should also be remembered that some of us had seen little or nothing of home since well before the war. I was sustained by the thought of my dear wife and of our little daughter whom I had not yet seen. I thought also of my mother, who, widowed in 1914 when my father was killed at the Battle of Mons, had brought up my sister and myself, and who was now so anxious for me, her only son. My father was a Regular and a Major in the Infantry when he went off to the war in 1914 and was killed. I too was a Regular and a Major in the Infantry, when I went off to the war in 1939 and had been captured.

I suppose death and captivity are both part of the profession of arms, although it is not a part which features much in the training we received as young soldiers. I had, in fact, read every book about escaping from the German prison camps of World War I and was therefore as well prepared as anyone for what lay in store for us.

There were those among us of whom it could be said, if not exactly benefitting from captivity, were at least able to 'keep their hand in' with their professions or hobbies in the camp. There were Doctors and Chaplins for instance. We had with us a doctor who before the war had been a psychiatrist. Here in Campo 29 he had about 175–200 human beings living under his close and constant observation, a human laboratory as it were. He gave us a talk once about his work and it was quite obvious that he was not wasting his time. He seemed to have us all taped and knew just exactly what made each one of us tick.

Some poor fellows went downhill because their home supports were knocked away. One heard that his wife and children were torpedoed and drowned in the Atlantic, while fleeing as refugees from their home which had been destroyed in a bombing raid. Others lost wife, mother, family or home in such raids or even worse perhaps, the wife did not wait for her husband's return, but went off with another man. When such a thing happened you could see the poor devil sinking before your very eyes.

We tried to occupy ourselves in many ways. There were lectures; I attended classes in agriculture, law, architecture (I designed my ideal country cottage in Campo 29) and I studied Italian. I also taught German. I chopped wood, did any kind of work, even the dirtiest, so as to keep up the idea of being a useful member of society, which was very necessary for me under those circumstances. The arrival of mail, books, cards and Red Cross parcels from time to time, relieved the tedium of the days, weeks and months. Before the winter arrived we received, through the Red Cross, battle dress uniform, warm woollen shirts, socks and underwear, a greatcoat and ammunition boots. The Italians wanted to cut holes in our jackets, overcoats, and trousers and insert large red patches to make us instantly recognisable as prisoners – like the broad arrow on the convict's clothing. But we kicked up such a row about this that they consented to sewing on a patch of red cloth which we could easily remove if we ever got out.

One of the best run and most expert services in the camp was the news service. There were two journalists in the camp and they were both absolute experts in reading between the lines – reading the news that wasn't printed. All they had to go on was the Italian press, heavily controlled and tightly censored, but they seemed to know how the Battle of the Atlantic, the Russian campaign and the battles we had recently left in the Western Desert or in the Mediterranean were progressing. Of course when the names of places we all knew well such as Mersa Matruh appeared in the press, where formerly Alamein had featured, no amount of writing about victories could conceal from us that the Germans and Italians had retreated some 90 miles. The only other sources of news were scraps to be gleaned from home and also from the arrival of a newly captured prisoner which was a rare event indeed. Yet these wizards forecast the North African landings and even got the date right.

I may say that we did a study of the invasion of Europe and my solution to the problem was almost exactly that adopted by General Eisenhower the following summer. It was uncanny and rather frightening to think that, if we could do it, cut off as we were from all sources of information, except those provided by the enemy, what must the Abwehr and the SIM, the German and Italian military intelligence organisations, have been able to do, who could listen in to our news broadcasts, read our papers etc.

The letters we received from home were all given to these two officers who extracted all the news of general interest and then they gave a talk after the arrival of the mail about life in England, the shows running in London etc, etc, which was of great interest. They also read between the lines as they did with the Italian papers and a good deal more than just the mood of the nation and government at home was gleaned from this source. Of course we had our good days as well as the bad. For instance there was the day when we heard in a letter from home that Lt. Col. Foote, DSO RTR,* who had been captured in the Cauldron Battle at the same time as us, had been awarded the VC. It was nice to know that we were not forgotten and that our services were not only remembered but also rewarded so dramatically.

I think the turning point in our lives was a momentous occasion when a new prisoner was brought in. It was at the time of Alamein whilst the Germans were still advancing and when our spirits were at their lowest ebb. He must have been struck by the miserable state of our morale for he addressed us all, in such secrecy as we could contrive in the camp. He was a New Zealander, Brigadier Clifton, DSO MC, who had been captured at Alamein only a couple of days before. He was square and stocky, of powerful build and ruddy with health and energy. He started off his talk with these words,

* Now Major General H.R.B. Foote VC CB DSO.

'Last Thursday I was talking to Mr Winston Churchill at Alamein.'

He went on to tell us of the build-up that had taken place and of the plans that were afoot to kick the Germans out of Africa. You can imagine the effect of his words. Our hopes which had been nil rose at a bound. Our captivity which had seemed likely to stretch away to an infinity of time was now suddenly shortened to something about which you could speculate, or even calculate.

Upon another occasion a tall Naval Officer, the Captain of a destroyer, Commander B.G. Scurfield, DSO OBE AM, whose ship had been sunk escorting a Malta convoy, walked into my cell before I even knew that anyone had come into the Camp that day, told me that he had met my wife and her parents and seen my little daughter about a fortnight before and brought news of home that was less than a month old. He had been told of my whereabouts by my wife and had jokingly said he would convey her best wishes to me if he met me, and here he was fulfilling his promise a good deal quicker than he had ever thought likely. He was taken away to Germany eventually and was killed at the very end of the battle in Europe trying to arrange a local armistice when the Russians met the British at the gates of his camp across the rotting remains of the German army.

There were the escapes too; they livened things up considerably. There were the weeks of preparation, and the precautions by those in the know, the deceptions, the watching and waiting and then 'the night'. Brigadier Clifton slid down a rope from a window which had been bricked up and which I didn't even know existed. He got clear away to the Swiss Frontier but was picked up in Como and returned in due course.

We had a tunnel through which several got out after months of difficult and dangerous work and the most ingenious arrangements and devices, lock pickings and deceptions. The subsequent alarms, searches, roll calls and even the sad return of the absconders some days later and the month's solitary confinement and their eventual transfer to a 'bad-boys' camp were all part of our life which gave us something to talk about.

The 'Last Post' was sounded at 10 o'clock every night and we all had to get out of the refectory and go to our cells and the whole of the ground floor became the domain of the Italians for the night. One chap had the idea of hiding under a refectory table and getting out, perhaps through the Commandante's office or by some other means. Unfortunately, he was spotted by an Italian patrol, who opened fire on him with his hands already raised in surrender. He was wounded in the hand and the fusillade in the confined space awakened the entire camp and stirred up a veritable hornets' nest of activity. The most useful and talented prisoner from the escaping fraternity's point of view was undoubtedly Major Clayton. I had met and worked with him in Cairo before the war, where he was employed with the Desert Surveys of Egypt. During the war he joined up and worked with the Long Range Desert Group; it was on one of their raids that he had been captured and was already a prisoner in Camp 29 by the time I arrived there.

As a Cartographer, Major Clayton could print anything and make it look indistinguishable from the original. This talent was put to use to produce forged passes, papers, certificates, etc. He did the printing and, if the document was in German, I wrote in the particulars in German script. In addition to this most valuable gift, he could pick any lock in the camp with a piece of bent wire, which enabled us to gain entry to some cellars from which the tunnelling party operated so successfully.

For money we were issued with paper 'camp money' with which items such as wine or vermouth (sometimes), fruit, razor blades and other small necessities could be purchased. The system worked as follows. Each prisoner was allotted so many lire a month and this was deducted from his pay issued in London. We often did not require to draw our allotment – there was little enough to spend it on after all. We each had a Pay Book and our credits and debits were recorded under the eagle eye of Bill Syme or Major Gurney. Many of us built up quite a credit with the Banca d'Italia at Piacenza, which we didn't have time to withdraw when we escaped from the Camp. I lost my Pay Book in Florence when I was recaptured there by the Italians and I was very angry when our Government 'would not' or 'could not' repay the balance which stood to my credit in Piacenza and I had to accept a token payment of £10 or nothing. I expect I've still got a credit in Piacenza: I must go there one day and cash it. I dare say it might pay for a cup of coffee.

This 'camp money' was only of any use in the Camp shop. The other currency, with which the contents of Red Cross parcels were bought and sold, was cigarettes. It was not a black market, if you wanted soap, butter or whatever, you paid in cigarettes or swopped other items which were valued in cigarettes.

In black market dealings with our Italian guards it was a matter of barter: they had eggs or fruit or something similar and we would offer them cheese, tea, butter, cigarettes or whatever they wanted and we could spare. One of the swindles in which we indulged was to sell them the tea leaves which the orderlies dried after use. Since tea, which came to us in Red Cross parcels, was completely unobtainable in Italy even second-hand tea was no doubt quite a luxury. Soap was another, and of course the inevitable packet of cigarettes, the most popular item.

I used to 'make' soap by collecting the little bits left over, dissolving them in water, and putting the slimy mess into a small tin to dry into a cake of soap. I also made soap flakes with an old razor blade, which sold quite well. I gave up smoking and sold my cigarettes for milk and butter with which to supplement my food and build up a stock of food for escape purposes.

The food we received from the Italians was the lowest of all grades of ration in Italy, and the quality of that ration was sometimes below what we would describe as fit for human consumption. When the Red Cross parcels started to come in, the Italian rations were improved by the addition of items from these parcels. The food was not memorable, and it caused many of us to vow that we would never ever again eat risotto – the variety of rice issued to us being pretty foul. I can hardly recall a meal at all, though I can remember dear old Admiral Cowan mixing the whole thing up together and mashing it all into one hideous heap and then eating it. He had lost his teeth when captured but this was no great loss for we had little enough to chew on. However, the quantity of food was adequate and nobody starved.

Water was always in very short supply, particularly in summer. The well at the back of the camp was totally inadequate and a mule-drawn water-cart was pressed into service to supplement it. I seem to remember that washing water was carefully preserved then used to wash down the floors; this in turn was saved and the murky remains would be slopped in small quantities down the squat-type latrines and thus we got by without disease or epidemic, although the results were somewhat odorous.

Apart from classes, debates, reading and such like, each had his own way of passing the time. One officer ran a carpenter's shop, another kept rabbits, another wrote a book, and so on and so forth. I had no particular hobby and I spent most of my time trying to do something active or useful, chopping wood, walking round and round the yard doing physical jerks etc to keep fit. We fixed up a net across the yard and played volleyball, and when the ball went over the wall we would shout 'Ballo prego!' and the Italian sentries would boot it back to us. Volleyball was pretty strenuous exercise and one game was about as much as any of us could manage on the meagre diet and in the restricted conditions in which we lived. When I visited the Camp after the war I looked into the yard through the little spy-hole the Italians had cut in the gate and there I saw the novices playing football in their cassocks just as we had played volleyball as prisoners. I asked if I could see my cell and the refectory and show my wife and children where I had been kept prisoner for nearly two years but I was told the Abbot was resting and could not be disturbed.

My main relaxation was reading the books sent to us by the Red Cross. I read and re-read Jane Austen, Trollope, Dickens, Thackeray, etc and was transported out of prison and back to England. Our Church Services had the same effect. I sang in the Camp choir and the psalms, hymns and responses took me back to the village church I attended with my mother and sister and brought a lump to my throat. I played bridge and chess, the light in the evening not really being good enough to read by, but you could see the cards or the board well enough.

I was quite good at needle-work and darned socks, made slippers and even made the hat worn by Squadron Leader Bax when he escaped. I also did cross-stitch work, the background of which was provided from unravelled grey army socks, but sadly these works of art all vanished when the exodus from the camp took place.

From time to time we were escorted on walks, by which means one got out of the camp and also got a little exercise. A column of prisoners would walk slowly about two miles from the camp. There would then be a pause and we would saunter back again. I used to go on as many as possible so as to get an idea of the countryside in the vicinity of the camp and also in order to keep as fit as possible. Keeping fit in body was quite possible, but the 'mens sana' part was not so easy.

How it was done I do not know but someone managed to construct a wireless set. I believe some of the vital parts came from the cinema projector which provided us with Italian films from time to time. With it we were able to listen to something rather more interesting than the local station.

I knew about the wireless set and I knew that they must have been receiving something in German because I was sent for to listen and translate. I hoped that we would hear a BBC broadcast to Germany or some stupendous news from London. I was all keyed up with excitement and expectancy as I crept quietly along the passage to another cell and then under the blanket which hid the set and muffled the sound of the broadcast. I put on the earphones and the epic news for which we had worked so hard was:–

'Ladies breaststroke 100 metres: First Fräulein Liza Schmidt'. It was Radio Munich but we did better later on.

Although my letters and parcels from home were a real life-line, I do not know what we should have done without our Red Cross parcels. They came from England, Canada, Australia and New Zealand. They contained mainly food, but we also had uniforms and warm clothing before that first winter and also books, cards and games.

When the food parcels arrived some items were removed and put into the kitchen to improve the general ration and the remainder was given to each individual to do with as he liked. Naturally we didn't want to consume the entire parcel in one go, so we put it into a store which was known as Tandy's after Major A.H. Tandy, R.A.S.C., a retired officer called up for the war, who ran it for us. I used to store such things as tins of cheese and butter in Tandy's in readiness for the day when I might get out. I also recall very clearly eating the curious tinned bacon after we escaped. We ate the meat and the rubbery rind and put the fat and grease on our boots.

From the window of our cell we could see, on a clear day, the snow-covered peaks of the Alps some 75 miles away to the north-west. This was a tantalising sight because those mountains were in Switzerland and were the goal of every escaper from the camp. It is perhaps a tribute to the Italian people that, although Switzerland was so close as to be visible yet a very large proportion of the prisoners when their chance came at the Armistice chose not the short comparatively easy trip to Switzerland but the route south to the VIII Army which was a very long way away indeed by comparison.

The passages in our wing were heated by terracotta stoves like the German 'Ofen', in which you burned bricquets. We burned wood. You lit a fire in the bottom and the warm smoke went up through the middle and upper storeys of the stove which were all warmed in this way. I was the camp wood chopper and some real tough gnarled old tree roots we used to get too. I therefore took charge of our stove and stored the wood under my bed so that it would be dry. We used to put a brick or stone on the stove to warm in the evenings and then stuff it into an old sock and put it in our beds to act as a bed warmer.

The winter of 1942/43 produced the worst weather we had to experience. The snow of February 1943 and the generally cold, snowy or wet weather all that winter meant that the guards refused to go out on escort duty on our walks. I dare say their boots let in the wet, and we were therefore even more confined to barracks than before for several months on end.

However, if the weather was bad the news we received that winter and the next spring was of the best and another little event occurred that gave me months of pleasure. A pair of goldfinches nested in the horse-chestnut tree in the courtyard and it was a joy to watch them feeding their young that summer. We missed them sadly when they flew away free as the air leaving us languishing still behind the barbed wire. But we were to follow them fairly soon and it was in this courtyard that the final drama of Campo 29 was played out.

III

FAREWELL CAMPO 29

'Last night you slept in a goosefeather bed
With the sheets turned down so bravely – oh
But tonight you'll sleep in a cold open field
Along with the raggle-taggle gypsies – oh'

Inside the yard all was quiet and still. The last of the prisoners had slipped along the path by the wall to his dinner. From his post between the second and third lines of barbed wire the Italian sentry looked into the yard, spat, scratched himself, and wondered for the thousandth time when this ridiculous war was coming to an end. Mussolini had gone. Mussolini had made the war hadn't he? Then why wasn't the war over? Why had the Government of Marshall Badoglio said with their first breath that the war would go on?

Inside the yard the five tall horse-chestnut trees looked down at the sentry as they had looked down at the novices and monks in the days before the barbed wire had been put up on those solid pine posts. Scattered about the hard-trodden patches which passed for grass were a few chairs, left out by some forgetful officers in spite of frequent injunctions to remove them from the yard before dinner. An empty wine barrel stood on its end by the door to the little room which was used as a canteen. A towel or two, a shirt and several pairs of socks were hanging listlessly from the shutter frames of some of the windows. The walls of the building held the still air in the yard, which had been warmed by the heat of the day.

It was getting darker now. The sentry outside on his beat shivered. Another hour and a half to go, and no greatcoat. The goldfinches that had nested in the chestnuts had long since departed, all that is except for the ones they had managed to get from the Carabinieri when they patrolled the yard at night. The fireflies had also ceased their short summer flirtations, which had seemed to try to mirror the glory of the heavens in the dirty grass which surrounded the camp. Another hour and a half to go: he would be cold; and afterwards – on duty all night – another go on sentry duty from two till three. How he hated going on patrols through the building at night. He thought he was being watched all the time, those English, they never said anything but . . . And that son of a bitch Sandro was back off leave, and would be out with his Paulina this evening. The dirty Naples dog. Oh, why couldn't he take Paulina off to his native Sicily – the war was over there. How he hated these stuck up stand-offish northern Italians, who couldn't even understand him when he spoke to them. He would kill Sandro slowly, oh so slowly, if he could only get him to himself in Sicily.

Inside, the yard it was so boring and dull, except for the low hum of voices, the subdued clatter of plates from the hall, and the feeble rasping of a cicada on one of the trees; there was no life, nothing to stare at, nothing.

In fact there was life enough. Too much life which had been lived too long and too close together inside the camp. It was a strange degrading life, a life of friends and friendships, and of antagonists and antagonisms, a microcosm of life with personalities impinging upon one another at close quarters for month after month after month. It was a perpetual battle against boredom which some never felt able to fight, or did not know they were losing.

The first hint of colder air from the hills kept the sentry moving slowly up and down to keep warm. It was about 7.15 in the evening and it was the 8th September, 1943.

On the southern side of the yard were the Italian officers' quarters and access to these was gained through a small heavily barred gate. This was being opened. The clunk of the lock, the muffled swearing as some invisible body wrestled with the bolt high above his head came clearly over the still night air. The door was at last opened and two Italians came into the yard. The sentry could only see the tops of their heads since he stood at a lower level, but by jumping a little he recognised the little interpreter with a face like a woman, and Sandro, that ever-to-be-damned Sergente. Ah, he was glad he had been caught for some job of work. He hoped it would keep him in all night.

As the door opened an orderly came to the dining room entrance to see what was going on. These Italians had a nasty habit of having a search when everyone was at dinner and not allowing anyone out of the dining room until it was over. No, this wasn't the guard, it couldn't be a search; he glanced quickly around the yard. The Interpreter was speaking to him:

'Please will the Senior British Officer come to the Commandante's office?'

'OK, I'll see, 'alf a mo'.

He went into the refectory, and delivered the message.

'Commandant's compliments, Sir, and would you go to his office.'

'Thank you Smart, tell 'em I'll come in a moment.'

The orderly returned to the door.

'He'll come in a minnit.'

'Can he not come now? He is wanted quickly, the Commandante says it is urgent?'

'Well you can 'ear 'e's talkin' to 'em; 'e'll be along in a sec.'

Inside the Dining Hall rumour was rife. Indeed never had Campo di Concentramento No. 29 been so full of it. The 175 plus Allied officers were mostly senior British officers between the ranks of Colonel and Major and they, in company with some 60 soldiers had been prisoners there for 18 months on average. During that time there had been many rumours but now they were flying around the tables thick and fast and one could follow their progress from the comments which marked their passage. Since the rumour was a very strong one to the effect that an Armistice had been signed, it is no wonder that it caused a stir even among the rumour-weary cynics who pretended to disbelieve it.

The hot watery soup had been disposed of and cleared away. A thin slice of meat roll with beetroot and a kind of sour endive was just being served, when the Senior British Officer (SBO) rapped on the table for silence. He did not have to rap twice.

He informed his attentive audience of the substance of the rumour 'in case any of you have not heard it'; and also the source thereof, which was a certain Lt. Col. Singleton, an old lag of great experience in such matters, who was generally regarded as the most reliable gleaner of information – though he had had a run of bad luck during the past fortnight or so when the mouth of the Singleton oracle had not opened.

'I have been summoned to a conference with the Commandante, and I have no doubt that this rumour may have something to do with the matter. When I have finished my excellent Canadian meat roll I shall go. In the meantime will you all please remain in or near the dining hall until I come back, as I may have something further to say to you.'

The hum of conversation rose a pitch or two after this announcement, so much so that the preoccupied diners hardly noticed that the guards were throwing their hats in the air, shouting, capering, weeping and embracing one another. As usual the prisoners had heard the news before their gaolers.

After a brief absence, during which every kind of opinion was aired and argued about, the SBO returned, and walked amidst a deathly silence to his seat. He did not sit down however, but remarked that since everyone seemed to be listening he would tell them in accordance with his usual custom the outcome of his interview. Were all the orderlies here? They were. The Officers turned their chairs round with much scraping and banging on the tiled floor. Those seated on the fixed benches which ran along the walls beside the long refectory tables twisted round or sat on the tables to get a better view of the proceedings. The orderlies were all clustered at the entrances to the room, and seemed to be more excited than the Officers, because some of them had witnessed the extravagant expressions of joy of the Italian soldiery.

'Well, Gentlemen, the Commandante appears to have heard the rumour too.' When the laughter had died down, he went on to add that a girl friend of one of the Camp NCOs was a telephone operator in Piacenza and she had told the Sergente that an Armistice had been signed in Rome and that Marshall Badoglio would broadcast an announcement at 7.30 that evening. He had suggested to the Commandante the advisability of getting some confirmation from the Stato Maggiore but they had heard nothing. In view of the fact that it was now 7.25 he suggested that everyone should go into the yard and listen to the announcement. Afterwards all ranks were to assemble in the dining hall for further instructions.

The clamour within gradually diminished as the Officers and Orderlies filed out into the evening air, where the noise was absorbed by the open space and the foliage of the chestnut trees, and overflowed softly into the ears of the Italian sentry. To him it seemed very odd. He had just heard the news a moment before from the Sergente. He had been so overjoyed that he had hardly been able to remember to curse the pig who had added that he had it from Paulina who had seemed very well when he saw her in Piacenza on his way back to Camp that afternoon. For him the war was over. There was peace again. He could now go back to Sicily. Why he was so happy he could even embrace that pig Sandro. What was the matter with these English? Why weren't they happy? Hadn't they any feelings? What astonishing people! Surely they should be more happy than he? The released prisoner should rejoice more than the gaoler who is merely let off his duties?

But the prisoners were prisoners yet, they were still behind barbed wire, and they were much nearer to Germany than to home, friends and families. They stood about in little groups, smoking, talking in subdued voices, their presence made more manifest by the glow of the cigarettes which added a slow pungent haze of tobacco smoke to the already scented night air, than by the sound of their voices. Some stood under the horse-chestnut trees, the trees in which the gold-finches had nested and the cicadas had sung that summer, others upon the paths round which they had walked (13 times round the yard to a mile) discussing life after the war, how to get out of the camp, religion, women and all the little things like sweepstakes, studies and comp-etitions which were run in the camp to while away the time. They also stood on the poor threadbare plots of grass where socks had been darned, knitting, backgammon and other unmilitary occupations had been practised in the summer sun.

The loudspeakers, fitted high on the wall to avoid any possible interference from us prisoners, crackled and spluttered. They had blared out the Italian news for over a year now, except for one occasion when an Italian soldier had been listening to the BBC on the office set and had carelessly left it tuned to the Allied frequency. Then the news had come loud and clear that the Allies had sunk a large number of German submarines in the Atlantic and Axis arms had suffered some appalling reverses in Russia, which not even the Italian papers had completely succeeded in concealing. The only other previous occasion when the Italian wireless had produced startling news of real interest to us had been a few days before when it announced, almost casually, that Mussolini had been deposed and that Marshall Badoglio had taken over. This announcement, despite a qualification that the war was to go on as usual, had been hailed with great jubilation by the Italian guards, with the possible sole exception of the fat little Fascist Caporale of whom even the Commandante stood in some awe.

The wireless cleared its metallic throat. The Italian speakers clustered more closely under the loudspeakers, and, as the announce-ment came through, translated it to those around them rapidly, phrase by phrase. 'Stand by for a special announcement.' Then followed a short statement to the effect, that, following the deposition of Musso-lini and assumption of power by Marshall Badoglio, Italy had surrendered and had concluded an Armistice with the Allies.

This poor little speech which was in fact a little piece of a gramophone record played in Rome, whence Badoglio and his Cabinet had long since fled, contained the news for which the prisoners had waited, some of them for years. Italy was out of the war, the Allies would now advance and would arrive at the Camp in a matter of days; soon after that they would be on their way home. No one at that moment considered the possibility that the Germans might have quite different ideas about all this, or that they could in fact do anything effectual in Italy without the Italians. In fact not even those who listened to the German radio that night, which spoke more truly than was its wont, when it said that all these events had been foreseen, that the necessary measures had been planned, and were even now being put into effect, believed that there was much that the Germans could do about it.

The prisoners took the announcement at its face value and gave a ringing cheer, which was answered by a storm of cheering from the guards quarters whence several caps came sailing high over the walls. From the dining room windows Italian soldiers could be seen hugging each other and dancing by the main gate and shouting to the inmates behind the bars.

To the renewed astonishment of the Italian sentry, the yard emptied itself rapidly of prisoners, who, in fact crowded excitedly back into the dining hall to hear further instructions from the SBO. The audience awaiting the SBO was charged with expectancy, they faced him a little breathlessly. The expectations, the thoughts and dreams of the last year or two had been fulfilled, they had heard the miraculous news and they looked to him to provide the miracle itself. Whether they expected parachutists to drop from the skies with tickets to Victoria Station, or an officer with an armband to appear from Genoa or Geneva or whatever, they did expect to be free and they expected something tremendous to happen.

The SBO was not slow to shatter these pipedreams. His speech was short and was to the effect that all were to remain in Camp. The situation was obscure, nobody knew what the Germans were doing, and several thousand prisoners loose in Northern Italy would add greatly to the confusion and might delay orderly repatriation. He had seen it for himself when his Regiment had had to clear up such a situation in Germany at the end of World War I. For this reason and because it was an order all ranks would be confined to Camp.

There were, however, a number of things that had to be done. Reserve rations which had been saved from Red Cross parcels for months against just this sort of possibility would be issued at 22.30 hours. A British inlying picquet would sleep in Room A16 to keep an eye on the guards and be ready to take over guard duty. All prisoners were to pack immediately and be ready to leave quickly and silently that night in the event of an alarm. All kit which could not be carried in an emergency exodus would be stacked in the cellars tomorrow morning. The life of the Camp was to go on, though under new management, and meals would be served tomorrow at the usual times.

A continuous watch had been instituted listening in to the BBC; news bulletins would be posted on Camp notice boards, and, if anything important came through, all would be informed in the shortest possible time. As from 07.00 hours tomorrow all ranks would be allowed to wander within a 1000 yards radius of the camp. An alarm signal and a bugle summons call were laid down. These points, given out in level matter of fact tones, were followed by a further appeal for good behaviour. All then sang 'God save the King'; and never was it sung with greater feeling and fervour.

For some time past the various Committees and the Floor Commanders had been in consultation with the SBO regarding the steps to be taken to cope with the kind of situation which had now arisen. Like the announcement on the German radio the matter had been carefully thought out and necessary measures were even now being put into effect. Reduced to its simplest terms the plans were to take over the camp either by force or peacefully, and to dispatch look-out parties to give warning of the approach of the enemy. No one could tell what was going to happen, a state of chaos was expected; but would it come before or after the Germans? In the present case neither had yet arrived, the prisoners had to remain in Camp and the Italian soldiers remained on guard. Nevertheless look-out parties were sent out on all approaches to the camp and a couple of prisoners were sent down to Piacenza, the local town, through which the Germans would almost certainly come. An inlying picquet was formed, sentries were posted whose duties were to look out for signals and to rouse the camp quickly to permit a quick get-away in the dark. The assault parties whose duty it would have been to overpower the guards and take over the defence of the camp if necessary, were also detailed and slept in a handy room so as to be ready to take over at short notice should anything happen to the Italian guards. A continuous watch was kept on the Allied Radio for orders but none were received.

After the singing of the National Anthem the prisoners scattered happily to their rooms and busied themselves in packing up the small accumulations of their years of incarceration. The camp was a hive of activity until a late hour, and, as may be imagined, those on duty were not the only ones who did not sleep. The tremendous news was talked over through the night by everyone. They spoke of home, wife or children in a new light now that the prospect of returning had suddenly become a startlingly close-at-hand proposition.

There was no incident that night and dawn found the camp already astir. A continual stream of prisoners came and went in the passages. Some carrying an assortment of packages, representing in some cases the work of years in various camps or perhaps merely the results of small self-sacrifices so that the prisoner could return with something to show for his wasted years of captivity. Some had written poetry, books, music, while others had paintings, drawings, and needlework, all hopefully labelled to home addresses. Yet others carried parcels of hoarded Canadian butter, Klim, the famous powdered milk tins, and slab chocolate with which to greet their family.

Breakfast was a hurried happy meal and soon small parties were wandering happily outside the wire, chatting to the farm people or the guards. A brisk trade was going on in soap, spare clothing and articles in short supply in Italy which were bartered for such things as eggs, grapes and money. A large party of cheerful workers set about improving the view from the front of the main courtyard by tearing down the posts and wire with their bare hands and what a difference those bleeding hands made to the outlook. Where previously sufferers from 'barbed wireitis', who had contracted their complaint prowling up and down like caged animals, there was a free open view of rolling hill and valley, access to which could now be gained by means of a wide flight of steps. These led down to an overgrown garden planted with young evergreen trees, doubtless, with the object of providing studious novices with shade in their perambulations.

The improvement to the view, which was certainly tremendous, was not, however, the only result wrought by those blistered hands and aching backs that hot, sunny morning. The removal of eighty yards of wire provided an excellent emergency exit for a large number of people in a hurry, and incidentally demonstrated the faith the SBO had in the discipline and self-control of the prisoners, since with the removal of the wire he could no longer confine large numbers to the area of the camp.

Everyone assembled in the courtyard at 11 o'clock to hear what developments had taken place in the situation. The Commandante had assured the SBO that the guards would defend the camp if it were attacked by the Germans, but no one was very impressed by this assurance. As a further concession to those who did not altogether trust the ability or intentions of the Italians, the SBO announced that those who wished to could sleep outside the wire, provided they remained in the immediate vicinity of the camp. The exact location of each party was to be reported so that all could be warned quietly in the event of alarm during the night. No news, orders or directions of any kind had come through during the night and a further disappointment now awaited them. An Italian officer had been sent down to the bank at Piacenza that morning in order to draw money in Italian currency with which to pay the prisoners the pay due to them, and to change the cardboard 'camp money' in which they had been paid up to the present. This Officer had returned with the news that the Germans were in control of Piacenza and that it was not possible to draw anything out of the bank. It also transpired that the Allied currency, which each had in his pocket when captured, and those articles of value which the Italians had impounded in their frequent searches had been transferred from the sequestration store to the Banca d'Italia only a few days before 'for safety's sake'. So that at a stroke the prisoners were deprived of their most realisable possessions i.e. gold and Allied currency, and also the pay they had saved. All would therefore be compelled to depart penniless from the camp when the time came to do so.

For the first time there was an air of disappointment about the audience. Why were they all confined to Camp and then left there without orders? Had the War Office or the Allied Command completely forgotten that there were over 50,000 prisoners behind the German lines, if there were any lines? Italy was plentifully supplied with mountains ideally suited to partisan warfare and an army or corps of partisan ex-prisoners would surely have been a headache for the enemy trying to run trains and motor convoys over his extensive land communications from Germany down to the front at Naples and Bari. The prisoners would not have been human if they had not complained, and many did so. They felt that they had been abandoned, forgotten, strangely enough both by friend and foe alike. In fact it was not until the evening of the 11th September when Mr Churchill's broadcast announcement as to the status of escaped prisoners was made, that any reference was made to them over the air.

As the afternoon of this peculiar day wore on, a trickle of refugee Italian soldiery started to flow into the Camp. They had come on foot over the fields and they were hot and dishevelled; some carried arms, some large packs of personal possessions. They were a rabble and looked it. To the prisoners their arrival was a considerable shock as it was their first glimpse of what had happened to Italy almost overnight. The nation had gone to pieces and here was proof. Here was the reason for the credibility with which even the most fantastic stories were received and passed on.

It was difficult to make them out at all. They were frightened; of what they knew not. They were on the march to the camp; why, none could say. In their shamefaced, fearful half-hunted looks were expressions that none of the prisoners had seen on the faces of their own soldiers even in the moment of defeat and capture. It was also a vision, although none of them were aware of the fact, of what their own appearance was to be in the months to come.

The unsettling effect of these runaways on the Camp guards was immediately noticeable. As a result the SBO gave special orders that the parties responsible for the protection of the Camp should be especially alert that night, and be ready to take over responsibility for the defence of the Camp from the Italians in the event of an alarm. It was as well that he did so for over two-thirds of the guards disappeared during the night.

The morning of, I think it must have been about the 10th September brought no news or instructions. The Commandante informed the SBO that in view of the departure of the majority of the guards he could no longer hold himself responsible for the safety of the prisoners. The SBO who had been the recipient of many schemes varying from a retreat into the hills en bloc, to a general assault on the German lines of communication in North Italy, decided, like Pharoah, that the time had come to let the people go. At the morning meeting he therefore announced his decision to let those who wished to leave, depart, but he also urged all and sundry to stay with the ship, and stated that he himself was remaining in Camp. The Camp would continue to function as long as possible and would be available as a base or supply point for any party or parties who needed help. The Commandante had by this time been able to get hold of some money and this would be distributed immediately against an entry in pay books. (The amount issued was between 200 and 400 lire, i.e. between ten shillings and a pound at the Allied rate of exchange.)

The Camp broke up amidst a scene of great activity. Some parties, all ready to go, simply picked up their packs and marched off into the hills behind the camp. Some, mostly loners, dashed off to change into their civilian clothes, and then made their way to the nearest station to catch a train or bus, or cadge a lift. Others started to carry away hoarded supplies to caches in the hills nearby with the intention of living in the district, while the majority formed a long impatient queue to wait for the Camp bank officials (British Officers) to pay out their ration of Italian currency. An early lunch was served at about twelve o'clock and by half-past-twelve, amid constant comings and goings, shouting of farewells, frivolous bets as to who would get home first, a continuous stream of prisoners started to leave the camp.

Everyone had their own idea about what they would do. Some headed for Como and those snow-capped peaks of Switzerland and safety, others were making for Genoa, which was not so far away and from whence they might take ship, perhaps to Portugal, if the Allies hadn't captured the place by then. Others made for the hills, deciding later what to do and some simply decided to stay near the camp.

Amongst those fleeing the camp that day was a group of eighteen or so of the younger prisoners. They had arranged a rendezvous about a mile up in the hills behind the camp where they would meet and decide their future plans. Most were quickly away, others delayed by last minute arrangements, and some like Bill Syme, the Camp Banker, could not leave until he had dished out the little Italian money he had been able to lay his hands on. I waited for Bill, helped him pack his last little treasures and we then set off after the others. On his shoulder was a pole from which various packs and packages were suspended. These swung wildly to and fro and this, with Bill's bad leg, made the going very difficult.

Soon after leaving the Camp the alarm sounded and we were soon sweating freely with various other groups in our attempt to advance as rapidly as possible into the hills. Upon our arrival it was unanimously agreed that a greater distance should be put between us and the camp and all straggled off to a secluded spot well hidden from the camp.

None of our party saw what happened when the Germans arrived at the camp. We were told later that they fired random shots into the surrounding woods, ransacked the buildings and failed to find a single prisoner. It was also said that Colonel Younghusband went round with the Germans pretending to be the Italian Doctor's assistant and that another officer, Colonel de Salis, who had hidden a large quantity of Red Cross parcels and some good books in a haystack just outside the wire, went and hid undetected in the stack like a broody hen, sitting on its eggs. He watched the whole performance from his rick-side seat as it were and then getting bored with the length and the Teutonic thoroughness of the search, he lit a pipe and set fire to his rick.

What stores the Germans left were taken by the local inhabitants or by wandering Italian soldiers, and nothing was found by those who went back later in search of provisions, books etc. Most of the prisoners who remained near the Camp hung on until the winter in the expectation of receiving some orders or of an Allied landing or some similar event. Then, when life became insupportable, they went to Switzerland, assisted by the most efficient underground organization which staged them through Milan, put them on the road to Como and the Swiss Frontier. Others joined partisan bands and some went to the coast or made their way to the south by various routes and means and, some of course, were picked up by the Germans or the Fascists and carted off to Germany.

Having found a good safe sheltered spot our party unhitched its packs and sat down in the shade of some scrub oaks to make up its collective mind what it was going to do with itself. Bill Syme set the ball rolling by proposing that I, as the senior regular officer present, should conduct the proceedings. It was obvious that eighteen of us could not wander together round Italy in battle dress and, as was already clear from the talk in the camp, nearly everybody wanted to do something different. I informed them that I intended to walk down the central spine of Italy, first to Florence and then south towards the Line in the hope of encountering partisans or parachutists in the mountains and therefore be in a position to take advantage of any landing or the chance of a submarine or boat which might take a small party off. Each was invited in turn to say what it was they wanted to do and so we grouped ourselves naturally into those wanting to head for Genoa, Switzerland, the south and those who proposed to wait around and see what developed. There were in the party some general duty men from the camp and these distributed themselves among the different groups.

Bill Syme, James Marshall and Trooper Maddox decided to come with me and so we broke up, each group making off in its chosen direction. We must have presented a peculiar picture, in battle dress from which the red patches had been removed, army boots and great coats with each carrying a pack or parcel and much else stuffed into our pockets.

In many of the best escape stories the hero is assisted by the gaoler's daughter, who lends him clothes, smuggles him out of the dungeon in a laundry basket and then is abandoned to her father's slipper whilst the prisoner meets friends who know the language and the country and rush him to the border pursued by the diabolical forces of the Secret Police, Army and Air Force and presumably the gaolers. Well none of this seemed to apply in our case, but it so happened that I did know the name and address of one person, my Aunt Eileen, who was living in Florence. Since she was the only person in the whole of Italy that any of us had ever heard of except the Pope and Mussolini, it was decided that we would make our way eastwards along the Apennines and try and get in touch with a fair rescuer, who, if she couldn't do the gaoler's daughter act, might at least be one of the friends who knew the language and the country.

Bill Syme was tall, pale and slim. He had a withered leg and a chest wound that had never healed. He spoke fluent Spanish and was a brave, cheerful soul with a loud infectious laugh. He wore a large rather 'Old Bill' type of moustache and was a little over 6ft. 2in. in height. James Marshall, a regular Seaforth Highlander, was fair-haired, strong and fit. He sported a large blond moustache and never managed to get to grips with the Italian language. Over his shoulder he carried a blanket, filled to bursting with Red Cross food and precious personal possessions, in addition to a pack and several Red Cross boxes and packages, the transportation of which slowed him up considerably. Maddox and I could easily pass for Italians, but as I was the only member of the party who had learnt Italian I had to do all the talking.

And so equipped we set out on a 500 mile walk, without map, compass, guide, friend or money, through completely unknown, enemy occupied, mountainous country, in the autumn, with winter approaching in a month or two. We had not gone very far before it was obvious that Bill Syme with his bad leg and James with that huge load on his back were going to hold the party up very badly. At length James threw down his load and declared that he could not carry it any further. The spoils were divided as far as possible and we hid two packages under a bush in case anyone might need them later on. It is to be hoped that some other prisoners, partisans or Italians found them, for none of our party was to pass that way again. There and then we decided to tuck in to James' surplus food supply and we ate an enormous evening meal, immediately encountering difficulties with the first tin we tried to open. If you ever have to escape from prison be warned – do not forget to take a tin opener! None of the three officers had thought of such a thing but Maddox had.

'Swiped it from the cookhouse, Sir, just before we left.'

After stuffing ourselves to repletion with James' surplus food all decided that our first priority was to put as great a distance as possible between ourselves and the camp while daylight lasted, and with James thus lightened we made better progress over the hills.

In the cool of the evening we cautiously bent our way down towards the Ponte del Olio valley through which ran the railway, road and a stream or small river. As we descended by a rough track we were greeted by Italians, girls, boys and old people who pressed grapes upon us and also invitations to celebration suppers, or even to stay over night. We accepted the grapes but felt it would not be wise to linger so close to the camp. We feared that news of our presence would get around and that we might easily be caught by a rastrellamento (cordon and search operation) which the Germans and Fascists could lay on with ease. These kind invitations were accordingly declined and we pressed on.

From what had become a triumphal march our progress became more furtive as the chill of evening and the smell of woodsmoke from farmhouse fires stole up on the evening air. We waited until dark and then crossed the river by a foot-bridge above the Ponte del Olio station, walked one at a time over the railway and road, and started up the opposite hillside sweating despite the keen night air, and did not breathe freely again until we had gained some rough ground well up on the far side of the valley. Here we found a dry ditch with a clear view all round with a few willow trees for cover in the midst of bare fields, gleaned of every blade of straw, over which we could observe the approach of any strangers. Wrapped in our greatcoats with the sweat drying on us we laid our heads on our packs and full of thoughts of what the future might bring and eaten alive by mosquitoes, my companions slept the sleep of exhaustion. But I could not sleep. The tussocks and tree roots made a hard lumpy bed and I was not yet accustomed to sleeping rough. Also I had plenty to ruminate on and my thoughts ran an endless paper-chase in my mind. My first thoughts were of my three companions. Maddox was tough enough. He had been an orderly in the Camp. He was a small, lean, wiry Lancashire man, who might have been anything from 27 to 40 years of age. He lay now curled up in his home-made sleeping bag with his pale craggy face partly hidden by the grey blanket. He didn't say much as a rule but there was plenty of sound horse sense in that hard knobbly skull. He had been a cotton finisher before the slump had put him out of a job and into the Army. He was a Regular and proud of it, and very well content with the life and wages in comparison with his experience of 'civvy street'. He had been blown out of his tank in the Western Desert some three years before and had been disfigured, giving his left eye a staring look. He belonged to that old-fashioned school which believed that all foreigners should learn English and he never spoke a word of Italian during the whole period we were at liberty. He was a great philosopher in his homespun way and gave a humorous slant to his opinion when he could be prevailed upon to give it. Maddox was alright. He could be relied upon. He would do as he was told, he would march fifteen miles a day and carry his load indefinitely. I did not waste any further thought on Maddox. It was the others who occupied my mind to the point of preoccupation.

James was OK but what about Bill? Bill Syme was a chartered accountant. He had been a very keen pre-war Territorial, who, to hear him talk was much keener on the Army than on his profession. He was a Gunner Major, which was no mean achievement, since his right leg was almost useless due to an attack of rheumatic fever long before the war. He was six foot two and was as thin as a lath. Besides his bad leg, which was sadly withered, he had been wounded in the chest before capture, and the wound had never properly healed. As a result he had a hole in his chest you could put your finger into. Over this he occasionally stuck a bit of sticking plaster. He had a high rounded forehead underlined by dark curving eyebrows. His dark eyes matched his manner which was cheerful and bright. He was in fact a most intelligent fellow and had travelled a great deal, though not, unfortunately, in Italy. He spoke fluent Spanish and talked a mixture of Spanish, French and English to the Italians who seemed to understand his meaning pretty well. Poor Bill, he had been on the verge of repatriation when the Armistice was signed but he never complained. He would probably be an enormous asset to the party; his loud hearty laugh, his zest for life and love of a joke would help when it might not be too easy to see a joke let alone enjoy one. But of course he would gum up the works if he fell with that leg in the mountains, or if his wound went bad on him.

James was a Regular Officer, and though of the same rank he was the youngest and the junior of the three, all Majors, lying there in the ditch. He was a powerfully built, well-proportioned fellow. He had a pale fresh complexion and an enormous moustache, and was indeed a credit to the Seaforth Highlanders, his Regiment and the Regiment of his father before him. He had a slow deliberate manner, which concealed an active mind and a tenacity of purpose which overcame all opposition when he had set his mind to a thing. Provided you didn't hurry James he would carry that enormous pack of his right past Doomsday to the Pearly Gates, but how in the name of all that's holy could you ever get James to resemble an Italian at even 500 yards range?

That was the problem for us all – how to look like Italians. How could we get civilian clothes. We were all four in some sort of uniform, some in the kit in which we had been captured, with perhaps here and there an addition sent out from home, or we were in battle dress obtained from the Red Cross. It was all undoubtedly uniform and clearly recognisable as such. The problem of how to talk like Italians didn't arise much at this stage, and James, quite a fair Italian scholar in the class in the Camp, had already proved himself a broken reed when it came down to light airy conversation with the locals.

Then there were the problems of tomorrow and the days after in the weeks ahead. How were we to feed ourselves? How were food, tobacco, soap, rations etc to be divided up and utilised, what was the best daily routine to adopt in this hot autumn weather but with cold nights and winter coming on? How far would Bill get? How far could you trust the Italians? Thank God we had got past that village and well over the road last night.

Before my thoughts trailed away into sleep and my subconscious mind started to grapple with fearful imaginary situations I wondered what had happened at the Camp that morning? How many had been caught? Did the Baron really hide in the haystack and bury his rations in a hole in the ground? But at last the great events of the last few days overcame the worries and anxieties. I smiled a great, wide, wonderful smile as I considered the splendid pattern of events which had led to our freedom and finally fell asleep in spite of the mosquitoes, the cold and the lumpy ditch, full of simple, solid satisfaction and of course James' surplus tins of food.

IV

'GIVE US THIS DAY OUR DAILY BREAD'

Our general idea was to make our way down the central spine of Italy, ready to take advantage of any development or landing on either coast or from the air, but very early in the proceedings our little group had to sit down and make up its collective mind not only what to do but how to do it. We were all agreed about making our way down the middle, which I called the 'Shade Way' after the great Scottish golfer S.D.B.M. Shade, who played the game so accurately and consistently that he was known as 'Straight Down the Bloody Middle Shade'. This for, 'Mr Shade' meant sticking to the smooth easy fairway, or in the words of the poet,

> 'Yon braid braid road,
> that lies across the lily leven'

but in the case of S.D.B.M. Mander & Co it meant choosing the hardest roughest and most difficult path imaginable,

> 'yon narrow road,
> So thick beset wi' thorns and briers.'

Next morning, thanks to the lumps in the ditch, the cold night air and the mosquitoes, we were awake early and quickly on the move, but the previous day's experience of the very hard going, the heat of the sun and our lack of condition forced us to think up a modus operandi. We decided that we would walk in the cool of the morning until it got too hot and we became hungry when a rest should be taken, if possible by a stream, and then we would move on again in the cool of the afternoon and seek out a safe place deep in the woods in which to spend the night. As Milton put it:

> 'Sweet is the breath of morn . . .
> With charm of earliest birds'

          . . . and sweet the coming on
     Of grateful evening mild.'

   We also decided that safety precautions were to be the top priority;
only rough tracks or no tracks at all, roads were crossed with great care
and a wide berth was given to villages and towns.
   And thus we wandered in the Apennines, in a general south-easterly
direction like a tiny splinter of a lost tribe of Israelites in the
Mountains of Moab, but with no tents, no flocks, no pillars of smoke
by day nor pillars of fire by night and no maps or compass either. In
the morning we set our faces towards the sun, unless it was shrouded
in early morning mist, at midday with the sun on our right and getting
uncomfortably hot, we rested, and in the afternoon and evening we
turned our backs on it and pursued our uncertain way until it was time
to find a suitable place to spend the night.
   We did, however, enjoy one advantage over the Israelites, our
Moabites were not only friendly but hospitable and helpful in every
way. But of course we did have to watch out for the Hivites and
Hittites in the shape of Italian Fascists and Germans, whom we
managed to successfully evade until we got to Florence.
   The local people, the Contadini, were peasant farmers, eking a
meagre existence in the mountains. They were unfailingly friendly and
at appalling risk to their lives and property offered us food and shelter.
Obviously we couldn't live indefinitely on the contents of our packs
and the few blackberries, nuts etc that we could gather; also sleeping
in the open, high up in the mountains was a very chilly and
uncomfortable way to spend the night. We wanted to keep in touch
with what was going on, so for many reasons we quickly modified our
routine aiming to get a meal at a farmhouse in the evening and some
kind of hospitality and food.
   Since I was fit and active and was only Italian speaker it fell to my lot
to range around, find out the best way ahead, find suitable isolated
farmhouses in the evening and talk our way in, and very hard work it
proved to be. I am afraid the strain told on me after a hard or bad day's
march.
   So it was very early in our journey that I left my companions
well ensconced in a deep wood while I set forth to see if I could find a
wireless set or get some news of what was happening. I found an
isolated house, a brick-built town house not a farm building, perched
on a ridge from which there was a marvellous view over the Po valley.

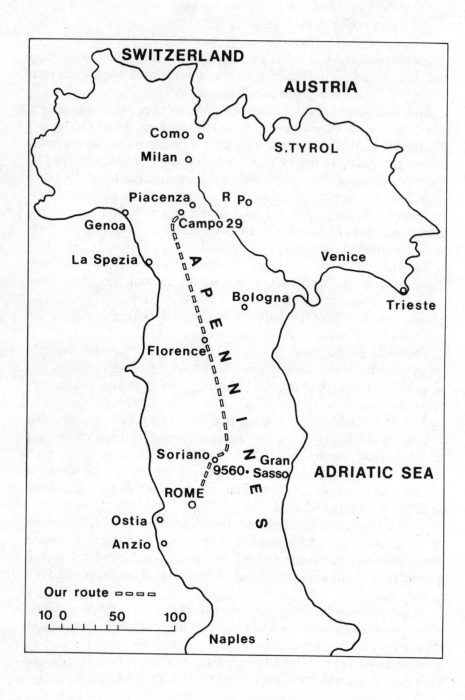

As I approached, I was greeted to my astonishment in English, with a strong Italian-Cockney accent, by a young woman. Before I knew what was what, I was embraced, led into the house, given warm water for a wash and sat down at table and then believe it or not she gave me fried eggs and bacon to eat.

I learnt that she had been born in London where she had spent her childhood and I imagine that her memories of English breakfasts led her to think that eggs and bacon were the staple food of the British. Her family had returned to Italy and lived in Parma and she had been sent up to their little house in the hills. Her husband was a prisoner of war of the British in Egypt. All this was poured out in a Niagara of words liberally larded with Cockney expletives picked up as a child, so much so that I called her Mrs Cripes. She was totally pro-British, anti-Fascist and anti-Nazi. She gave me some of her husband's clothes and a hat. We sat and listened to the BBC news in English on the wireless and she wouldn't take a penny piece or even a cake of Palmolive soap by way of payment or as a present.

It was therefore a long time before I made my way back to our camping place in the woods, where I found the other three in a very worried state. They thought it was unwise of me to contact the locals and feared that I had been recaptured or got lost. They had hidden my pack and were on the point of moving off deeper into the wood when I reappeared. Their worry and upset over me brought me down to earth with a bump when I returned in triumph from my little adventure.

This disagreement was the first we had had since we left the camp but it was not to be the last. It stemmed from over tiredness and anxiety. Over tiredness in my case and anxiety on their part. In defence of my short temper I can only plead that having suffered the full rigours of each day's march, I then undertook the scouting out of a suitable place at which to eat and spend the night. Having found it, I then had to talk our way in, tell the family about our homes in England, show them photographs of children we had never seen, tell them how far we had marched that day and answer their questions. In this matter of answering their questions I found that I represented the Allies and had to explain why the BBC had said this or that, why the Allies hadn't bombed the local railway junction which was cluttered with German equipment, why the Allies hadn't landed on the Brenner Pass at the Armistice, why they were so slow in their advance etc etc etc. This was hard work indeed especially to people who spoke differing dialects and it proved to be great strain on me making me snappy when my arrangements were criticised or questioned. I felt the burden of this lay almost entirely with me, although Bill's flow of Spanish–French–English and his ready laugh helped a great deal.

Sometimes I would be led some miles away in the dark to a house where, in an atmosphere of the greatest secrecy, we listened to the Boom Boom Boom BOOM of the BBC news and I would have to listen to Mr Grisewood's cultured tones muted to the utmost for the band of conspirators gathered to hear it 'from the horse's mouth'. Here again the news would be of the Salerno battle, bombings and bombardments by battleships, bridge heads, holding out against furious German attacks but there never seemed to be any progress in our direction, no landings up the coast or on the Brenner and invariably I had to translate it into Italian and I was asked why, why, why?

There was another matter which I have never understood to this day. There must have been thousands of prisoners in the Po Valley, between 150,000 and 175,000 were in camps scattered about north and central Italy. From our experience we knew that the vast majority of the Italian nation, including their armed forces, police etc were on the side of the Allies. Why weren't all Allied prisoners ordered to leave their camps, take to the hills and arm themselves with Italian weapons? Why were the Italian army not appealed to in the same way? If the instruction had gone out to get organized, get a wireless set, get ready to go into action; surely those thus mobilized could have cut every crossing over the Apennines and others could have done the same thing on the line of the River Po and all the way down Italy wherever prisoners had been held. Would not such operations have been able to hold up supplies at vital moments, could we not have held down many German divisions, which were at that time being deployed in the south? How could they have fought as they did if the British and Italians in the north and central Italy had taken to the maquis in September 1943? Why were we told to stay in camp and be good boys, many to be sitting ducks for the Germans to round up at their leisure?

In the BBC series about SOE (Special Operations Executive) operations in Italy which was broadcast recently (Winter 1984/85) we heard that the SOE had managed to get one intrepid Major across the Ponti Vecchio and into Florence in August 1944 – nearly a year later – when the Germans had retired from Cassino to the line of the Apennines. We had about 200 there a year before. Why I wonder were we ignored, abandoned and indeed in some cases handed over to the Germans on a plate?

However to return to our march through the Italian countryside. My experience with Mrs Cripes and our meeting with the Italians as we were leaving the rendezvous to cross the Ponte del Olio valley changed our ideas on the subject of living on the food in our packs and sleeping in the woods and from then on, at the end of our days march, I would set out to find a suitable remote farmhouse and then talk our way in to some kind of meal and shelter for the night, and here I must emphasize the great help that the brave, generous and hospitable Contadini gave us. We were scarcely ever turned away, and if we were, there was always some good reason for it. We always got something to eat and generally some bread for the next day. For shelter we slept in hay-stacks, cattle sheds, with pigs and with donkeys and I can tell you that cattle give off the most warmth but the plop plop plop in the night and the smell of ammonia made for disturbed nights and a headache the next day. Pigs are the best and donkeys the worst sleeping companions. But the Italians lock up their livestock and, as escaped prisoners, we did not take kindly to being locked in at night, in the hands of people we did not know and so we graduated to fienile (hay barns) ricks or even deserted huts which often had a good heap of dry leaves to provide warmth.

Hay or straw was lovely and warm and nobody locks it up. But you have to hang any food from beams with string or the rats will eat it. They also nibble your feet and run over your face at night, which can be most unpleasant.

We used to leave a note or chit with the household so that when the Allies arrived they would know that these people had helped us. (See copy reproduced on p.46.)

There were also in the woods charcoal burners, who, whilst no doubt perfectly willing to help us, had no food or shelter and could not even direct us to the nearest farm or village, because we could not understand their dialect.

The priests varied enormously. Some were most helpful and kind but most simply said 'Go to the Contadini', and gave us no help whatever.

> 'The rich man in his castle
> The poor man at his gate.'

We poor beggars found that the rich people we met were not, as a rule, helpful. They had great possessions and could easily lose them

From Major Mander.
Major F.J. Syme
Major J.M. Marshall
Tpr J Maddox

The people of this farm have given
us food and every assistance they
could when the Germans occupied
North Italy and we were prisoners of
war at large.

Mander
Major
No 44/31 The Green Howards

This chit was left with the Gandolfini family at Boccolo Bardi near Parma. Their son Angelo Gandolfini sought me out in England and told me that his parents' house had been razed to the ground because 'they had sheltered Parachute Troops'.

In recognition of what they had done and suffered on our behalf I was able to recommend them for the Field Marshal Alexander Certificate and for assistance from the Italian Government with the rebuilding of their house.

whereas the Contadini had little to lose and they shared what little they had with us and we can never thank them enough for what they did for us.

We often found upon our arrival in some remote locality, that Signor So and So was the man to see, and having found him, or he found us, we would be addressed in English, often almost incomprehensible English. There was one fellow for example, who had left his village and gone to the Shetland Islands where he made and saved his money, returning a relatively rich man to become the squire of the village. His Scots-Italian flowed all over us and we had to converse with him in English or he would have lost face with the villagers. Mrs Cripes was a Cockney, another chap had sold ice cream in the valleys of Wales, another spoke American/Italian and in each case these individuals had established themselves as the leading citizens of the community, not only because they could speak English but also because of their knowledge of the world and their money.

The farmers generally gave us some sort of evening meal and bread for the next day. We often left very early in the morning or in the night, in case our presence had become known and we might be the recipients of the '4 o'clock knock' on the door. Sometimes after such a move, we might call in at a farm further on for a bowl of milk for breakfast or else subsist on the bread we had received.

We gathered blackberries, wild pears, chestnuts and in the stubble we often saw where the odd potato, which must have been left in the ground from last year's crop, was growing. These we grubbed up with our fingers and cooked either in our cooking pot or in the ashes of our camp fire with the chestnuts. There were also grapes to be had. And so it was that we made our way through the mountains. We acquired a cooking pot and a billhook and one Italian family had given me some little maps the size of playing cards out of a 1910 Baedecker Guide with the aid of which we set course for Florence, Rome and the south.

We did not worry too much about getting to a given point each day, our main object was to remain at liberty. In all things we put safety first. If there was any argument as to which course of action should be taken the safest course would be adopted.

Occasionally we would hear rumours that the Allies had captured the Brenner Pass, or held all the crossings over the River Po, landed at La Spezia or Ravenna. We continued on our way in the hope that one day one of them would turn out to be true.

The BBC News which we tried to listen to as often as we could in the hope that we might be given some idea of what was expected of us, contained many 'special messages', 'The Eagle has landed', 'The horses gallop', that kind of thing. I suppose they related to the dropping of arms, explosives or agents but none of that sort of excitement ever came our way. On two occasions we were told that a boat or submarine would be coming to some spot on the coast and that we could be picked up and we were ready to make a dash to the coast but in each case a great 'paura' (a terrific panic) set in and all was cancelled, given away or something and we set forth on our way as before.

I had noticed that the Italians went out into the fields barefoot, just in shirt and trousers and I foolishly tried to do likewise with the result that whilst squelching along in deep mud I got a nasty cut in my right heel which went septic and became badly swollen. Then Bill, whose chest wound had held up well until now, was laid low and this was a serious blow because we were the only two who could communicate with the locals. But as luck would have it we had arrived in a secluded valley where we had been made universally welcome and where we felt safe from any surprise visitations. The chief personality was Signor Cavalli (Mr Horses of the Welsh valleys) and he took charge of us. He had a large farm house but turned out to be somewhat tight-fisted. However, he was a man of authority in the valley and through his good offices and the kindness of the Contadini in the farms round about we were supplied with our daily needs.

We lived in a deserted hut, which was half full of blown leaves, but it provided us with shelter and some warmth and there, by means of the warm milk and the meals which were brought to us, we were able to recruit our spent forces. I called the place Vale End.

The autumn was turning to winter, the nights were getting decidedly chilly and rain made sleeping out in the woods regularly something to be avoided. But the more I was laid by the heel the more restless I became. I did not like sitting still in one place where everyone knew where we were and as soon as I was able to put my foot to the ground I wanted to be up and away. I started scouting around for alternative accommodation, in case we had to make a quick move, and exploring the surrounding hills and forests. But before taking our departure from this part of the Apennines I would like to describe what happened to some of my friends who stayed in the area of the Camp, went to Genoa or made a break for Switzerland. Those of us who went south and got away re-joined the VIII Army whilst the war was still going on. Those who made it to Switzerland were able to keep in touch with one another but were unable to get out until the Allies reached the Swiss border in 1944/45, and of course those who were re-captured and taken to Germany, were not released much before V.E. Day in 1945. Several had interesting tales to recount.

My Australian Battalion Commander, Lt. Col. Cooper; Lt. Col. Bush, 5th Green Howards; Lt. Col. Norman, 4th East Yorks and Lt. Col. Reynalds, who commanded 44th Bn The Royal Tank Regiment, together with Major Tony Dobson the Brigade Major, all got to Switzerland by means of a 'Guide Line' and under their own steam.

The first escaper from our camp to reach Switzerland went to a very crowded hotel for a meal. When he got there he was asked by the Manager if he minded sitting at a table with some Italians. Having no objection he was shown to a table where he sat down to lunch with the Commandante of Campo 29 and his wife, who had just beaten him to Switzerland by a short head.

Major Tony Dobson,* left the camp with Major Stephen Radcliffe and was soon offered shelter by a friendly Italian family. They were hidden in a barn full of maize stalks by day emerging only at night for food and air. The family were well-to-do folk. They were Roman Catholics and of course anti-Fascist. They were, however, very critical of the Pope, who they said could have stopped the war if he had exerted himself.

There was a scare one day when the owner of some car wheels, which were hidden under the maize, wanted them back and they had to spend the day in the woods whilst the wheels were retrieved. From the woods they could see Campo 29, it was occupied by German troops and a very great deal of activity was going on.

So they decided to move higher up the mountain where they found shelter with some very poor but kind people. During the weeks they were there the only meat eaten was one squirrel, which did not go far between five large members of the family and two escapers.

From this haven in the mountains Tony busied himself, with Lt. Col Boddington,† a Sapper Colonel from the Camp, collecting,

---

* Major Dobson, subsequently the late Major General A.H.G. Dobson CB OBE MC, recorded the story of his escape to Switzerland on tapes, which are now lodged at the Imperial War Museum in London. This account is a short extract from these tapes and is published with Mrs Dobson's permission.
† Lt. Col. N. Boddington OBE Royal Engineers.

feeding and transporting escapers to Switzerland. The Italian side of this organisation was run by a chap who was known as 'The Gangster'. He had a garage and hired cars to the Germans and he was paid by means of chits signed by the escapers, but he was rumbled in the end and eventually he was shot by the Germans.

After working for Colonel Boddington for about three weeks Tony decided he would like to make a move himself as the weather was turning very cold and life in the mountains was getting pretty bleak. However, the Colonel informed him that he was under his orders and was required to stay and continue his work on the 'guide line'. Having referred the problem to another senior officer from the Camp, he decided to leave and was assisted by some smugglers who were trading tobacco for saccharine over the Swiss frontier.

He was kitted out with a new suit, shirt, tie and hat and also with a pencil. Apparently all respectable Italians carry a pencil! Together with two middle-aged Italians, who were operating a wireless set for the partisans they set out for Switzerland. The Italians had lost their cyphers or the code had been changed and they were bound for the British Embassy in Berne to get new code sheets. They boarded the train at Piacenza and travelled to Milan. On arrival in Milan they had to walk across the town to a different station, buy another ticket and wait for a considerable time before the departure of their train to Como. In Como they found themselves confronted with large numbers of Italian soldiers and had to walk right in front of the local military Headquarters on their way to the lake-side where they boarded a boat which was full of school-girls on an outing. They disembarked at Menaggio further up the lake and immediately had to climb a steep cobbled track to a house where they were met by the wife of the man who was to see them over the frontier the next day. Suddenly the husband appeared and told them that they could not stay there but must go to the house of his Uncle and they set off again on a steep 2000ft. climb to another house where they spent the night.

Early next morning, before dawn they set out for the frontier. It was late October and it had been snowing, they were escorted by the little Italian in Bersagliere uniform. The frontier, when they reached it, proved to be a 10ft. high chain-link fence topped with barbed wire, a formidable obstacle for tired, cold, wet and out-of-condition escapers. However, the Bersagliere, whose job it was to stop people from crossing the frontier, but who in fact received L50 for everyone he escorted over it, lifted up the fence, and they crawled underneath it.

He threw their belongings, wrapped in a handkerchief, over the wire, presented arms to them and waved them on their way.

They were quickly picked up by Swiss Frontier Guards and escorted to a Quarantine Camp at Chiasso, where the Swiss wanted to shave their heads and fumigate their clothes. They managed to persuade them that it was contrary to the Geneva Convention to shave an officer's head, but their clothes were fumigated and Tony's new suit shrank to about half its former size. Since they had arrived in Switzerland in civilian clothes and were not armed they were treated as 'évadés de guerre' and were not interned. If you arrived in uniform, with weapons or in a military aircraft you were interned and not released until the war was over. Tony was sent to Arosa, where he was able to ski and, travelling up an anchor lift with a fair young Swiss maiden he struck up a conversation with her in German. His German must have been pretty good for she soon became Mrs Dobson!

The poor fellow who had the misfortune to share a cell with me for 14 months had no such luck. Major Dennis Whitehead MC TD of the 5th Bn The Green Howards, was one of those who decided to stay in the mountains near the Camp in the expectation of a landing at La Spezia, Genoa or on the Brenner Pass. He left the Camp on 10th September 1943 with four members of the East Yorkshire Regiment.

They, like us, lived at first in the woods on the Red Cross items they had taken from the Camp in blankets slung over their shoulders. But they also soon found that the Contadini were friendly, hospitable and helpful and they got into the way of coming down from the tops as night fell for a meal, spending the night in a barn and making themselves scarce the next morning with a hunk of bread or a piece of polenta for food.

However, they quickly realised that five hungry men descending upon a poor little farm house for a meal was to ask more than the Contadini were able to provide, so they split up and Dennis Whitehead paired off with Captain D.E. Field of the 4th East Yorkshire Regiment keeping in touch with the others by day. They quickly built up a circle of friendly folk in their area and visited different families willy nilly each night so that the others never knew where they were and no-one could be accused of harbouring them. They exchanged their battle dress uniform for a motley collection of clothing, the quality of which may be judged by the fact that a dismantled scarecrow provided a portion of their wardrobe.

When the expected landings at La Spezia etc did not materialise they decided to sit it out until spring rather than go to Switzerland and face internment. But with the advent of colder weather, conditions for them and their Contadini hosts became more difficult. Quite a number of their friends had made their way to Switzerland with the help of the 'Guide Line' and in November they got a 'Come along' message from Lt. Col. Foote from Switzerland to say that the guide line was good and that he and several other officers from Campo 29 had arrived safely in Switzerland, had avoided internment and hoped to be able to get back home via France and Spain.

So they changed their plans, got in touch with the guide line and set off on 22nd November to meet their guide. Arriving at the rendezvous they found no less than seven ex-Campo 29 Officers were there ahead of them, one of whom was Major Bill Bailey,* who was all of 6ft. 3in. in height. Since the trip was to be a daylight train journey to Turin, the Italian guide pointed out that Bill's outstanding physique would attract attention to the party and suggested that he should go on the next trip with Dennis Whitehead and Captain Field, which was to be at night. On the evening of 25th November, the three of them set out for Piacenza with a lady guide. They were to take a workmen's train to the frontier near Turin, where they would arrive early in the morning and lie up there the next day ready to slip over the frontier at night.

At first all went well, but they became separated and, when crossing a long bridge at Bettola they ran into a posse of Italians under the command of Tenente Zanoni, who, thinking they were deserters from the Army making their way home, arrested Dennis and Bill and marched them off to the Town Hall at pistol point. Captain Field and the guide had reached the train safely, but when Zanoni realized that Dennis and Bill were British, it dawned on him that Captain Field must have been one of the party and he rushed off to grab him off the train and claim the handsome rewards that were offered for capturing ex-prisoners. In fact he picked up Captain Field and four other escapers who had already reached the train and were to make the trip that night.

While Zanoni was away Dennis and Bill were guarded by one of his minions who sat at a desk with his pistol pointed at them. They sat on chairs about 12ft. from the desk, and Dennis thought he would see what the man was made of, so he got up, walked up to the desk and draped his scarf over the pistol and resumed his seat. The guard put

* Major L.S. Bailey RASC T.A.

the pistol down on the desk and started looking through the papers and their belongings which had been taken from them and were lying on the desk.

'We could make a go at getting out of this if you agree' said Dennis. Bill did agree.

'I'll sweep the pistol off the desk and look after himself and you get the gun.'

As they went into action the guard saw them coming and grabbed the pistol but Dennis forced his arm back and Bill seized the pistol. Dennis spread-eagled the fellow on the floor and Bill held him covered while Dennis scrabbled about collecting their property which lay in chaos on the floor. Bill then told the guard in good old English soldierly language not to bloody well move for five minutes and they rushed out into the night with the pistol and their belongings, leaving the office in chaos, with the typewriter broken, ink on the ceiling and the filing system in ruins.

They made their way out of the town and set off as fast as they could for the mountains from whence they had come. They were soon completely lost and very footsore and weary when they suddenly recognised some barns as being the home base of other prisoners with whom they had kept in touch, and who were due to take the guide line the next day. They dropped in for food and shelter, warned their friends that the guide line was not functioning, spent the night there and made their way back to their own area the next morning.

Soon after their return they learnt that Captain Field and his four companions had been picked up on the train and that Zanoni had put about a story that Dennis and Bill had killed the guard, which was not true, and was offering millions of Lire as a reward for their re-capture. They realised that if they were discovered it would place the Contadini who had sheltered them in dire trouble and they decided that they must at all costs have another go at getting to Switzerland. However, this was becoming increasingly difficult and Dennis and Bill split up to spend Christmas with their Contadini friends, but renewed their efforts to get away. Eventually they got in touch with the local black market king, who said he would take them in his lorry to a guide in Piacenza, who would escort them over the frontier.

This young fellow had a lorry with a pass for the transport of wine, and of course much other black market produce, about the country. They met him at a deserted spot, got into the lorry, hid among the wine barrels, and were driven directly to Piacenza and into a yard full of Italians with rifles under the command of Tenente Zanoni!

The man was obviously after the reward, but all he got from Zanoni was a kick up the backside. The men in the yard with Zanoni were civilians, armed with rifles and seemingly half-drunk. Zanoni marched Dennis and Bill into the moat, stood them up against the wall ready to shoot them. Luckily at the last minute he called off the execution, frog-marched them into the citadel and down to some underground dungeons where they were locked into the condemned cell. On the way in Dennis caught a fleeting glimpse of Colonel Arthur Robinson, an anti-aircraft gunner from Campo 29, who was cleaning his boots by the guard-room machine gun.

That afternoon Dennis was taken from the cell for interrogation in Zanoni's office where he was punched and beaten up with a knotted raw-hide whip. His spectacles were removed before the beating which was prefaced by the ominous words:–

'Don't mark him.'

He was then told to get out and seeing his spectacles lying on the desk he walked up, retrieved them, put them on and as he walked towards the door, he was given the most tremendous kick up the backside and made a flying exit from the office.

That night they banged on the walls and shouted into the ventilation duct and managed to get word to Colonel Robinson and tell him of their dire predicament. The Colonel told them that the Germans were coming to collect him the next day and said he would get them to take Dennis and Bill away as well.

The next day, when the Germans arrived, Zanoni, who had a bad reputation with the Germans for ill-treating prisoners, denied that they existed, but Colonel Robinson persuaded them to search the place and get them out. Dennis had never been so pleased to see a German soldier!

After about a fortnight in German hands at Parma together with two South Africans, two British other ranks, two Russians and one Chinese, they were put into cattle trucks and commenced a long, slow journey to Germany dodging Allied bombing raids. They were detected trying to saw their way out of the cattle trucks on the Brenner Pass and, after another week in the trucks, being shunted about in marshalling yards, they arrived in Offlag VIII in Czechoslovakia. There a massive break-out was blown by a British RASC Captain, and the camp was surrounded by a battalion of fresh troops in the middle of the night after which they found themselves the next day in Offlag 79 near Brunswick in the middle of Germany. They were liberated some fifteen months later by the American Army on 12th April 1945 and were flown home from Brussels in C 47 Dakota aircraft.

On arrival back in England, Dennis reported Zanoni's conduct in considerable detail, but he heard eventually that he had been shot by his own people, which saved everyone a great deal of trouble.

V

'LEAD US NOT INTO TEMPTATION'

'The Signora of Monte Verde'

To return to our valley, christened 'Vale End'. My heel got better relatively quickly, but Bill took longer to recover his health. We were adequately supplied from the little community below and when I was laid up, Maddox or James would go down and fetch the bowls of food or warm milk and the bread with which those kind people supplied us. Sometimes a polenta or other dish would be brought to our abode by young people who were anxious to see us and where we lived.

Soon the old restlessness returned to me and with it the urge to be out and about getting to know what was going on around me. As soon as I was able to walk any distance, I went straight up into the woods to look for a refuge in case we had to leave Vale End in a hurry. High up at the top, I came across a group of charcoal burners, who were curious people quite unlike the Italians we had as yet encountered; living in rough huts they built great mounds of cut saplings, which were burnt with very little air thus producing a fine black charcoal. They were black-haired, dark-skinned, gypsy-looking people and the blackness of their skins was further darkened by the smoke from their craft and handling the charcoal (and the lack of water and all or any sanitary arrangements so far as I could discover).

There was also another difference, they were not as friendly or generous as the Italians with whom we had so far been in contact. Since I could not understand their speech and they were very poor it may have been that they had nothing to offer or give. Certainly, I do not think they would have given us away to the authorities. I went on over the top of the mountain and came to a considerable village or small town. Here I received a friendly welcome and for the first time I ventured into a town, went into a shop, talked to the people and was everywhere received with kindness and generosity.

But however kind one's hosts there was always the danger that one's presence would become known and someone might give you away. Even in this out of the way place there were people in uniform –

Carabinieri, bus drivers, postmen and, most dangerous of all, Guardia Forestale (armed and uniformed state forest game-keepers) all minions of the Fascist state, and how could I know if they were to be trusted? As a source of money and supplies this place was wonderful but as a place to stay – no.

As I descended to the town I saw rising from a jumble of hills to the south a solitary peak somewhat higher than the surrounding hills. It was not its height which attracted my attention but its size and remoteness. The sheer bulk of its steep sides, clothed at the bottom with trees and shouldering its way upwards amid a pathless wilderness with the main mountain range solid behind, it gave an impression of security and safety and I therefore decided to trek there the next day.

Of course I did not tell anyone in the town about my companions, where I was living or where I had come from and in the same way I did not mention to anyone where I intended to go the next day. After a pleasant meal in a friendly house I retired for the night to a barn a short way up the hill to which I was guided by a boy well after dark. He unlocked the door and when I was inside he made to shut the door and lock me in. I relieved him of the key and assured him that I would constitute myself the guardian of the hay for the night. When he had left I let myself out, locked the barn door and sought such shelter as I could find in the woods.

The next morning I returned the key and after a good breakfast, with a hunk of bread and some cheese in my pocket, I skirted the village and set off towards the mountain which was called Monte Verde. It lay some ten or fifteen miles or so to the south east and must have been an old volcano so regular was its conical shape. Thick woods encircled its broad flanks like a grass skirt, the peak rising bare above the tree line. There seemed to be no roads or tracks emerging from the woods and, as I later learnt, only shepherds and their sheep were to be found on these slopes in the summer. It looked like an ideal place of refuge to me, the tracks were too steep and rough for transport, and men who knew the country would never be caught by soldiers or Carabinieri in the tangle of wild hills at its back.

It wasn't long before the wind got up and clouds came scudding across the sky hiding the peak from view. A thin rain fell alternating with heavier showers. I debated whether to go on or return to my friends of the night before, but the mountain had made such a strong impression on my mind that I pressed on, with the wind and the rain mainly at my back. I was soon soaked through and, as I climbed up the mountainside, the sweat on my vest mingled with the rain making me even wetter, if that were at all possible.

As I climbed its western flank I saw a few scattered farmhouses to which I gave a wide berth. They were isolated enough but not quite what I was looking for. Leaving them well to my left I went on up through the woods and came suddenly upon a remote farmhouse beside which a rocky track descended presumably to the community below.

As I moved on up and round to get a better view of the place a bullock sled came lurching and squeaking down the track loaded high with hay, straw or bracken. A small figure was perched on the front of the sledge urging on the oxen, he was wearing a sack over his head and shoulders as protection against the rain which was now falling heavily. On approaching the house the figure hopped lightly down from the sledge and drove the oxen expertly to the barn door.

'A grandfather', I thought and a pretty nippy one too. I was hiding in the wood over-hanging the track and as I jumped down on to the track and announced my presence the grandfather nearly jumped out of his skin. But as I approached I realised I was talking to a woman and a fine young woman she was too. She set about unhitching the oxen and unloading the sledge of bracken single-handed.

I apologised for startling her and commenced my usual long explanation, which was obligatory in the process of getting somewhere to shelter for the night, she quickly cut me short.

'You alone?'

'Yes.'

'I see to the beasts, you put bracken in the loft.'

I took a light wooden three-pronged hayfork and pitched the bracken into the loft, buckling to, full of curiosity, but content to give her a hand. When I had finished pitching in the bracken she told me to take some wood into the house and get the fire going. Taking some firewood, I kicked the embers together and soon had a good fire going. I made several journeys and soon had a good pile of logs by the fire. I then went to the byre and carried in the milk while the mistress of the house shut up the outhouses and came to the house with a small lantern and inspected me. I must have been steaming in front of the fire, for she said:

'Oh, you are wet to the bone – clothes all off.'

I stripped off my clothes and sat by the fire in my underwear. She reappeared with some warm underwear, a shirt and sweater which all seemed somehow to be hundreds of years old. I put them on gratefully and draped my sodden garments over the bench while she went to another part of the room to prepare a meal.

'Can I wash?'

'Over there.'

I found a stone sink and washed in the cold mountain water, afterwards standing my feet in a bucket to numb the soreness of the day's march. I returned to the fireplace barefoot and luxuriated in the warmth.

From the kitchen area came a series of questions: who was I, from where? etc etc, and I told her about my companions, our plan to march down the Apennines and rejoin the Allies, which was greeted with snorts of derision and I was given a lecture, which I had heard so often before, to the effect that the only good Italians were the Northern Italians, to the south the farms would get bigger and the owners would not welcome us and anyway people down there were not to be trusted. She brought me a glass of red wine.

'You stay here tonight?'

'Is permitted?'

'Is permitted.'

She went back to the kitchen and in between bouts of furious activity she asked me about my family, my companions and our experiences in Italy so far, repeating her warnings of the difficulties that lay before us and said we should stay there where we would be quite safe. The other three could be accommodated on other farms on the mountain, it was obvious that I was invited to stay with her; I repeated our wish to move on and rejoin the Allies.

She told me her name was Rosa. She asked if I had passed any other farms on my way, and I told her I had come up through the woods well away from the little settlement lower down.

'Good, then you can sleep here – no need to hide away in a hay loft.' She brought a nice hot supper which we consumed with more wine and she told me about herself. Her husband was missing in Russia. He or her family owned much of the land round here and she had come here from Siena, where she had a house, in order to keep the farms going.

After supper with my clothes now dry and folded away we sat in front of the embers of the fire into which a drop of rain fell now and again causing it to hiss and spit at us.

'Why not stay here? Is very safe here. You helped me today. I need help. I am at the end.'

I suppose I was the first able-bodied, Italian-speaking, ex-prisoner she had met and I was more or less the answer to the maiden's prayer. However, I told her that I couldn't hide in the hills and let our friends fight their way up while we did nothing.

'Well you can join the partisans on Monte Bianco and between battles you give me a hand here.'

I told her I didn't think much of the partisans I had seen so far and that we were all determined to press on south. She said that without help, she would have to shut up the house with the arrival of the snow, move all the beasts to other farms lower down and go back to Siena. She was composed but on the verge of bursting into tears and had she done so I am sure that I should have taken her into my arms and comforted her, then perhaps my story would have taken a rather different turn. As it was she picked up the candle and showed me to my room. There, stretched between the cool sheets in the first bed I had slept in since leaving camp, I had much to think of and perhaps also much to dream about.

Next morning, as usual, I awoke early, slipped on my clothes and crept down stairs. I quietly raked together the fire, put water on to heat and went outside. It was still dark but the sun was rising over the Adriatic and its light, as though from beneath the earth, unearthly, lurid, faintly tinged the clouds with a weird pinkish-purple luminosity. The light grew stronger, a small breeze stirred the tops of the trees. I shivered. Back to Vale End after this! As I went back into the house, a blazing log tumbled out of the fire on to the stone hearth as if to remind me of the warmth of my welcome of the night before.

Just then Rosa came down and told me that I could stay in bed a while longer if I liked, she was going to milk the cows, and she clattered out to the cow shed. I washed and shaved thinking what a marvellous woman she was and what a prospect I was throwing away. Then I went out to the byre to give her a hand with the animals and mucking out and carried the two foaming buckets of milk back into the house.

She made us some acorn coffee with the milk still warm from the cows and we ate a slice of bread.

'You stay here now? Is no good in the South. You and your friends will be safe here.'

'I will go back to them today and I will tell them what you say and if they are well enough, we will come here tomorrow night or the next day.'

'If you go down the track ask at the farms. They have a cart which goes to get supplies and perhaps you can ride back.'

Rosa wanted to send in her produce and also to order some salt and other supplies, so she walked down with me carrying some large baskets of farm produce and she arranged for me to go in the cart. When I protested that this was not wise she said:

'They will know you have been here. They know everything.'
And it was quite true. I had been seen in the woods and my destination had been correctly guessed. Rosa was quite unconcerned. I said a rather stiff and starchy goodbye, climbed into the cart and clip-clopped off briskly to the town which we approached quite quickly by an unmetalled road.

My driver, Enrico, had been told to say nothing about me and drop me off out of sight of the town and so I was soon clambering down, waved goodbye and set off cheerfully into the woods, circum-navigating the town and was quickly round the hill and at Vale End.

Upon my arrival it was obvious that, left to themselves, my companions had made up their minds exactly what they wanted to do and that was to get on the move again and continue our march steadily south. Since this was my idea originally I could say nothing to the contrary.

'All mended and well, Bill?'

'Good as new; we ought to be on our way. I don't think we should impose on these people any longer and we're getting to be a bit too well-known around here. We've had some visitors I didn't like the look of yesterday.'

'Well I have found a super place where we can stay tomorrow night anyway.'

And I told them of my friendly reception in the town and about Rosa and Monte Verde.

'Sounds OK to me. Will we make it in a day?'

'If we leave bright and early we ought to make it easily and if we don't we can easily find somewhere or other to lie up for the night.'

That evening I went up to Mr Horses to say our goodbyes and also down to the farms which had been supplying us with food, and of course I was told we would be much safer here and how dangerous it was further south etc etc etc, but I explained that we had decided to move on and I left chits so that they could show them to the Allies as proof that they had indeed assisted us that autumn. We had a farewell supper at one of the farms, not Mr Horses' you may be sure, and after pressing invitations to stay and many warnings of the difficulties and dangers that lay ahead we went back to our miserable hut and turned in on the leaves which had been our bedding for the last few days.

Although I knew the way and was confident we would make it to Monte Verde quite easily in one day we decided to make an early start and thus avoid any farewell delegations and arguments. So at about 4 a.m. we set forth and were well on our way before daylight, which had been our normal habit in the past. The day's march was routine and we arrived tired but comfortable enough by mid-afternoon. Rosa met us at the farms and my three companions were distributed among the farmsteads while I went on up with her to her little house.

It was immediately obvious that she had by no means given up the idea of us staying on Monte Verde and she elaborated plans whereby we were to be accommodated at various farms and she spoke of shepherd huts, high up on the mountain top which we could use as refuges and of course all the arguments about how impossible it would be for us to continue further south. She had prepared a special meal for me and it was very hard for me to have to explain that we had all made up our minds to continue our march. I could only add lamely that she could ask the other three and she would get the same answer.

I was quite used to interminable arguments and warnings but this evening proved to be a most severe trial. After all in Monte Verde and at Vale End we had found two almost ideal places in which to stay and I could only promise, that if the difficulties and dangers ahead proved to be too much for us, we would come back without fail to Monte Verde.

'You must come before the snow. I cannot work the farm in the winter. I send the beasts down to the farmsteads and I go to Siena.'

'Could I come and visit you in Siena?'

'Is no food in Siena.'

Eventually I retired to my little room and again stretched myself luxuriantly but sadly in the bed and slept.

The next morning before dawn I was up and helped with the animals and the fire. At breakfast Rosa put out a few more ideas about our staying in the area, joining the partisans, etc and I said we would talk about it when we met the others, knowing full well what their answers would be. We went down to the farmsteads and there we met Bill, James and Maddox, full of praise for the kindness and warmth of the welcome they had received but still firmly decided that our march should be resumed and it was more or less, 'Thank you very much indeed. Goodbye and when do we start?' And with many last minute directions and warnings we set off through the woods in the general direction of Florence.

VI

FLORENCE

The reader may well have been given the impression that so far our progress along the Apennines from Piacenza towards Florence had been a pleasant stroll, a series of picnics followed by a fireside supper in a farmhouse. Of course, in comparison with the experiences of the Allies, fighting bloody battles all the way up from Calabria across innumerable valleys each defended tenaciously by the Germans, I suppose that is what it must appear to be, especially perhaps to any members of my old battalion who may read this story.

To us, however, it was far from being a picnic. In the first instance, thanks to our own insistence of putting safety first, we always avoided the easy way, the wide valleys with roads, villages, railways and so on. We took to the hills and chose the wildest, roughest and remotest tracks. We walked along the northern flank of the Apennines where they run from west to east opposite the Alps on the other side of the Po valley. This meant that we had to cross many valleys which had been cut by the streams running into the River Po to the north.

In September, although during the day the sun was very hot, we were high up in the mountains and at night it was very cold which, as I have already mentioned, caused us to get into the way of finding isolated farmhouses and begging shelter for the night. Early morning sometimes found us enveloped in mist, we could see nothing, we had no compass, it was far too cold to sit around and wait for the fog to clear so we blundered about to keep warm until the sun drove the mist away. The valleys were steep-sided and high up they tended to be either rocky or thickly wooded and the woods were sometimes full of brambles and very nearly impenetrable.

Eric Newby describes in his book *Love and War in the Apennines* how he wanted to climb up to the spine of the mountains and have a look at the west coast in the direction of Carrara and so he must have been quite close to where we found ourselves after leaving Monte Verde. He hoped to make the climb and return to his hiding place the same day. He already knew part of the way as he had lived in a shepherd's hut on the tops for a while. He had been given detailed directions, he had a sketch map, food and plenty of warnings and he set out with a march table in the autumn. It nearly killed him. He got to the top but, coming back he lost his way and got stuck in one of the bramble-filled woods, eventually arriving by great good luck, at a farmhouse, lacerated by thorns, minus half his trousers and jacket. He got back a day or two later to be greeted by his friend.

'You've been the hell of a long time. You look as though you have been trying to swim the Channel.'

They never tried to move again from their hiding place and, when the snow came, they were picked up and taken off to prison camp once more.

Well, we encountered similar problems. Up to now we had been walking along the northern slopes of the mountains, but in order to head for Florence, we had to go over the tops and continue along the southern flanks, and it suddenly became apparent why we should have paid more heed to the repeated warnings we were given. The going got worse, the farms almost non-existent and Bill with his bad leg and James with his heavy pack began to find the going very difficult. Such places as we found were extremely poor, very small and primitive and simply could not accommodate or feed all four of us. It became obvious that, whereas two would be welcome, four were not. It was decided that, as Maddox and I were much more active, we should split up and we therefore reluctantly left Bill and James to pursue their way at a slower pace thus permitting Maddox and I to forge ahead rather more quickly. Looking back I think the decision was correct, that what we did was right and there was probably no alternative. But it is still a decision that gives me cause for bitter regret, for after my return to England I learnt that Bill and James were overwhelmed by an avalanche in the Gran Sasso and both were killed. The Gran Sasso is in the mountains to the east of Rome. How they managed to get so far that winter, I have no idea. It must have been an heroic effort.

One morning, on leaving a friendly and most helpful family, we enquired how best we could avoid a village which lay in our path, and we were directed to go over a hill, down into the valley on the far side where we would find a mule-track leading to a hydro-electric station where we could find our host's relatives and a warm welcome.

We gladly followed these instructions and, after a short climb and much slithering and sliding down through the steep wooded slopes on the far side, we found the mule-track which led off in the right direction and set out on a rocky path, which wound its way ever higher up the valley for about 14km until at last the power station building came into view. It was a stark, tall, square concrete tower built into the side of the valley on top of which were the quarters of the engineer-in-charge. It was a veritable fortress of a place with a wonderful view of the track we had just come along but there was no exit at the top of the valley, which was completely enclosed by mountains. It was the sort of place I am sure that in a Holywood epic Errol Flynn or Clint Eastwood would have defended against the entire German Army with ease.

The engineer's daughter, the niece of our friends of the night before, came out to meet us and when I told her where we had come from we were accorded a warm welcome. The engineer was an elderly man who lived here with his daughter in what must have been the most lonely existence imaginable, dependant as they were upon fortnightly visits by a muleteer from the village about 19km down the valley for supplies and local gossip. There was no need here for me to talk our way in. As soon as they knew we had come from their relatives we were most cordially invited to come and stay the night and later that evening we were pressed most earnestly to stay permanently amid the usual warnings of the difficulties that lay ahead which were drummed into us again.

Indeed in this case it was most difficult to leave as we were at the head of the valley and the way ahead was barred by the peaks of the Apennines with no road or track over them, the only obvious way out being the way we had come in. Certainly if I had been single and alone and had not wanted to get back to our side so badly I could have settled down there safely and most agreeably for the winter.

The next day I explored the mountain barrier ahead of us and began to wonder if we would not indeed have to stay where we were or go back the way we had come as there seemed to be no easy way out. However that afternoon we were introduced to the Guardia Forestale who we asked to guide us to the top of the mountains and put us on our way down the other side. This he readily agreed to do. This news was received with dismay by our kind hosts and we were regaled with more warnings of the perils which lay ahead, to which we could only reply that if things became too difficult we would make our way back to them, but if we made it over the lines we would send a Messaggio Speciale 'Meriela sta bene' – Meriel is well – so that they would know we had arrived safely.

The next morning the warnings and pleadings were repeated, but we said our sad farewells and resolutely set off to the meeting place we had arranged with the Guardia Forestale and took our departure.

That day's march was the hardest that I remember, but we succeeded in climbing out of the valley to the very top and descending the equally steep and difficult slopes on the far side and made our way along the southern flank of the mountains finding shelter and pursuing our way towards Florence.

As Maddox and I approached Florence one last obstacle faced us – the Bologna to Florence valley, with its very busy road, used mostly by German military transport, its railway and river. We crossed the valley in the evening, and waiting for a lull in the traffic, we were able to cross the road by means of a small bridge or culvert which ran under it. We nipped across the danger spots one at a time or tried to stroll unconcernedly along in places where there was no cover and where furtive behaviour would invite interest. At last we climbed up the far side with a feeling of great relief and so it was that we arrived in the hills beyond Fiesole on a warm afternoon in late October.

Here the mountains, the steep valleys and the forests we had become accustomed to, gave way to rounded hills upon which stood palladian farm houses with fine avenues of cypress trees. There were roads and well-kept farm tracks aplenty and the farm houses seemed larger and more prosperous-looking than those of the Contadini, whom we knew and trusted, some even had electric light. We sat on a bank overlooking the city lying at our feet to the south; I pondered how we would ever be able to find safe houses or good lying up places in such an area. I also wondered how on earth I was going to be able to get in touch with my Aunt Eileen.

'What do you think Maddox. Shall we try one of those big places? We might do a bit better than last night.'

Maddox's craggy face broke into a rueful smile.

'We'd best stick with the Contadini, Sir.'

'Rather the rats than the Germans, eh?'

'Well, I can't say as I fancy their cold feet on my face and when they start nibbling my feet, well there's something to be said for the glasshouse.'

'Right, Back to the hills – no fleshpots for us.'

And we set out with the usual problem of finding somewhere to spend the night. No sooner had we got to our feet than we were hailed by a sturdy, handsome young woman, who invited us to her house for a bite to eat. We gladly accepted her invitation but quickly saw that this was no place to spend the night. It was a small house which stood right beside a good unmetalled road. The farm was a small holding and the man of the house was called in from his work in the field to meet us. He too was quite young and seemed well fed, but they were obviously poor folk and could not possibly have had very much by way of food to spare. But they were a mine of information and obviously in full sympathy with the Allies and, despite the proximity of the road and the view of Florence below, we felt quite safe with them.

The story they had to tell was a peculiar one. There had been one or two Prison camps for British other ranks in this area and the prisoners had worked on the farms during the period of their confinement. As usual the British soldiers had endeared themselves to the Contadini and when the Armistice was announced they had walked out of the camps and had gone to live with the Contadini for whom they had worked or whose handsome daughter had caught their eye. These poor people, who had been feeding many POWs for some time, had now run out of food and wine and had come to the end of their tether.

Our host pointed out a farm, high up in the hills behind, where he said thirty POWs were being fed. We thanked him for the food and for telling us about the local situation and I promised to go to the farm he had pointed out and see if I could do anything to sort out the problem.

We set off in the direction of the farm he had indicated but when we were out of sight, we made off in another direction and sought more secluded shelter for the night. We soon found what we were looking for in the shape of a large farmhouse lying in the middle of a wide valley, well hidden in oak woods which were still in full leaf and hid it from view completely.

Here again we were made welcome and the same story about the POWs in the area was once more poured out to us. When they heard that I was a Major in the British army and learnt that I could speak and understand Italian it seemed to be assumed that I had come there solely for the purpose of resolving their difficulties.

'Signor Maggiore, something must be done. Some of the Contadini are starving and they cannot keep their 'boys' any longer. Soon there will be a denouncing and the boys will be arrested and the Contadino will be shot.'

A feast was ordained and some children were sent out to catch a turkey. Maddox and I went with them and with some difficulty caught and killed the turkey which we brought back in triumph to the house where it was summarily plucked, disembowelled and in the space of less than a quarter of an hour it was in the pot. When all were assembled for dinner, there proved to be quite a company of adults and about six children belonging, as far as I could see, to two sets of parents. There was also a pocket Hercules of a man who was installing electric light in the valley and the celebration tonight we discovered was not at all in our honour but because today they were to be connected up and switched on for the first time.

'Hercules' carried the poles on his shoulders from the road, straight across country, up and down hill, digging the holes, planting the poles, attaching the wires all entirely single-handed. He was a most popular fellow and was full of jokes and fun.

'Now Adriano no more kissing in the dark. With the electric light Mama sees it!'

Adriano, a gangling youth who had obviously been caught or suspected of kissing one of the younger girls about the place blushed to the roots of his hair.

'And you, little Patrizio, must wash the face better because Mama will see the dirt now.'

'And, Signor Elettrico, you will not have to look out for the foot of the bird on your plate.'

After a happy supper, and with the children fast asleep on the floor we talked over a glass of wine, and the seriousness of the situation was brought home to me.

'Tomorrow Signor Maggiore you will talk with Father Bonomi and you will see,' said Enrico and I replied, 'Well, Enrico, Soldier Maddox and I are marching to Salerno and perhaps we can take some of them with us.'

That night, comfortable and replete, in a nice little shed some way from the other farm buildings I had much to reflect upon before sleep overtook me. I viewed the prospect with some misgiving: I would be the only officer in the area which might contain hundreds of POWs. I would have to order them out and would have no backing to my authority. I had troubles enough of my own without having a battalion of POWs wished upon me.

Next morning I was taken to see Father Bonomi in the village which lay at the far end of the valley perched upon a shoulder of the hill before it emptied itself into the Arno below.

The Father quickly made the gravity of the situation plain to me. He estimated that there were about 1500 POWs in the area and unless over 1000 were moved quickly he did not know what would happen. An educated young man called Gianni was assigned to me as a guide and assistant and with him I met many of the prisoners and visited most of the farms where they were living. I quickly learnt that the person I would have to deal with was a Guards Sergeant Major of whom the inhabitants stood in considerable awe. He was indeed an imposing figure, being about 6ft. 4in. tall and thin as a lath. He wore his regimental cap and a long army greatcoat and it was quickly obvious that he saw no reason why he should move out of his comfortable quarters or indeed pay any attention to a scruffy little person who called himself a Major in a Line Regiment.

I had served with Guards Regiments and had observed with the greatest admiration their discipline. This was based upon the efficiency of the officers, especially the Warrant Officers; guardsmen, however, had to be shouted at before they would move, and I had a shrewd idea that the Warrant Officers and NCOs had little respect for the rest of the army. I explained the situation to the Sergeant Major who was evidently unimpressed.

'You come 'ere, been 'ere five minutes and now we all 'ave to shove orf. Oo the 'ell do you think you are layin' dahn the law etc etc etc. . . .' I lost my temper, I was absolutely furious. There seemed no point in starting a slanging match so I hit him very hard in the middle of the last four buttons of his greatcoat and caught him another on the jaw as he doubled up. He went down but not out, however, he stayed down.

'Want any more?'
No answer.

'Very well if you are not away from here by tomorrow night I will come and repeat the dose. Father Bonomi will help you with addresses to go to and provide a guide to start you on your way. I am sorry I had to hit you but this is bloody serious.'

I hauled him to his feet and he drew himself up, replaced his cap, stood to attention and threw me a fantastic salute.

'Very good, Sir.'

He turned smartly to his right and marched away. Gianni and Maddox had watched the proceedings speechless.

'Now all goes well. When the Sergente Maggiore goes all will go,' said Gianni.

'Dunno about that!' said Maddox, 'bloody drain pipe! 'e might come over wiv some pals of 'is and kick us aht o' the place.'

'Then you and Signor Elettrico will have to be my body guards and Elettrico will knock him down with one of his poles.'

But I think the Sergeant-Major had realised the force of my words and knew in his heart that things just could not go on as they were for much longer and with the others he went like a lamb.

Leaving Maddox at the farm, I went with Gianni to the village where we reported progress to Father Bonomi, who needless to say, had heard it all already and was busy arranging a series of posting stations, guides and even transport for the prisoners. Whilst busy with these details a girl came into the room and was introduced to me as a member of the local underground movement in Florence. Her name was Robin. When she started to talk about her work and life in Florence I asked her if she would be able to find my Aunt Eileen. She seemed to think she would probably be well-hidden but, I gathered that finding people who are well-hidden in the underground is not too difficult provided you are a member of said underground. With that she departed by bicycle and I stayed the night in the village well satisfied with my day's work .

Whilst engaged on the task of moving those ex-POWs on, they inundated me with questions. I was the first British Officer they had seen since they had been captured.

'Sir, how long can we go on?'

'What about letters? How can we write home?'

'What is happening in the war? At home?'

They could not speak or understand Italian and just did not know what was going on. They obviously missed their letters from home, the rations and routine of Army life and wanted to write themselves. I could only say that the best thing would be to march south and rejoin the VIII Army as soon as possible, and that anything was better than being in prison.

We were greatly assisted in our task of persuading the men to move on by a Rastrellamento in the area. A line of Carabinieri formed up at the foot of the valley and advanced like beaters to a row of stops at the valley head. Everyone found in the area was to be questioned and men of military age or POWs would be picked up and arrested.

Before the Caribs appeared, however, everyone seemed to know what was going to happen and by the time the line of black, red and white uniformed men had spread out across the valley and started the beat, all the POWs, partisans and Italian absconders were on the hill tops watching the proceedings with interest and amusement. After a rather perfunctory operation, in which they found nothing at all, they gathered on the little road at the head of the valley where the stops had been placed, got into their transport and drove back to Florence, all the better for a day in the country and reporting, I hope, that the area was clear of POWs.

Robin had sent a message to say that Eileen had left the address I had given and the people there did not know or were unwilling to say where she had gone. Since there seemed to be little chance that I would be likely to see her and as the situation in the area was now much more healthy I decided to go over to Monte Morello where, I had been told, a similar POW problem existed. There were, in fact some 150 POWs in the Monte Morello area and I managed to get them moving; dispersing them in much the same way as I had done the other side of Fiesole.

I well remember going to one farm where Signor Brancalone, his wife and two grown-up daughters were feeding and accommodating no less than seventeen POWs. Gianni had told me that they had now run out of food and wine and Signor Brancalone had gone down to the town, got drunk and poured out his troubles for all to hear. It was this incident which made the whole community afraid; if the Fascists or Germans heard and came to the area and found any prisoners, the punishment was death and the buildings would be razed to the ground. I explained to the POWs and Signor Brancalone the danger and difficulties of their situation, pointing out that the POWs must move on. On hearing this Signora Brancalone burst into tears.

'But they are like my sons; we love them, they must not leave us.'

'But you cannot feed them. You will all starve and then they will have to go. Think of the danger you are all in. It is better for them to go now than in the winter.'

'But not all?'

I repeated my warnings about the dangers of being caught with prisoners, but they were insistent that they could feed and keep two well concealed. So Signora Brancalone chose her two favourites and the other fifteen left with Gianni and I. Unfortunately, I never found out what happened to them all. I had intended to follow in their footsteps and act as sheepdog along the long road south but fate was to decree otherwise.

However, I did hear what happened to the Brancalone family. After we left the authorities visited the Brancalone farm and caught the two POWs. I learnt the sad news that Signor Brancalone was shot before his wife and daughters, the barn set on fire with the livestock in it and razed to the ground.

During my stay in the Monte Morello area I met a band of so-called Partisans. They appeared to me to be a bunch of very young, very left wing communistic young men who had got hold of some pistols and were chiefly engaged in raiding the shops and homes of the Fascists, which may have been a bit of a nuisance to the authorities but they were neither armed nor trained to do any useful work, such as cutting telephone lines, blowing up electric power pylons, railways or road bridges and they were quite obviously never going to be able to take on the German or the Italian Army in any kind of guerrilla warfare. I felt that if we were ever to get down to organising an ambush and the firing started I would more than likely find myself alone and that they had all scarpered!

I met them in a barn at night and whilst I was there some of the band returned with shoes and stockings, the result of a raid that evening on a shop in the local town. Since I rated their military value as zero I decided to walk back past Fiesole as soon as possible and to see what news Robin might have for me about my Aunt Eileen.

I also met the Pastore family of Monte Morello who owned a Ceramica factory in Florence. They were totally pro-British and were looking after three South African officers whom I had also met. Signor Pastore went in to Florence every day and brought us news of what was going on in the city and he also had a wireless set on which we could listen to the BBC in the evening. I remember we also discovered a small overhang under a low cliff which we tried to improve into a cave for an emergency refuge, but none of us was much use as a cave builder and we gave up the attempt, but I did sleep in it whilst over there.

On my return from Monte Morello I heard from Father Bonomi that Robin had found my Aunt Eileen and I was told to be at the little farmhouse, where we had been so kindly received upon our initial arrival, at midday the next day. As usual we took our normal precautions. We arrived well beforehand, and found a spot from where we could see the rendezvous unobserved.

'Maddox,' I said, 'She won't know me from a hole in the wall so why don't you get up and give her a smacking kiss and set yourself up with an English girl friend in Florence for the rest of the war.'

'Ah would an all if they 'ad any char, but we haven't been doin' too bad lately.'

'OK, Maddox, let's see what happens.'

We soon saw Robin's long-legged figure walking up the hill with another woman. When we established that they were alone and nobody was following them we stood up and walked down to the road. Eileen rushed up to me and exclaimed at my resemblance to my uncle, her late husband. She was very pleased to see us, and had brought us cigarettes and money. We went into the farmhouse where she spoke fluently in Italian to our hostess, and indeed I was reduced to English by the flow of her words. She also obviously enjoyed speaking English to English people once more, a pleasure Maddox and I shared and enjoyed. I presented her with a packet of tea which I had jealously guarded for this occasion and Eileen insisted in broaching it there and then, instructing the farmer's wife in considerable detail as to how it was to be prepared and served. The farmer's wife, much impressed with the Signora from Florence, produced some excellent refreshments of a sort we had never before been offered, and these we ate with great relish, washed down with a cup of real tea.

Eileen had many enquiries to make and was full of plans for helping us. Our boots were removed and taken to be repaired. I was to have false papers to enable us to travel on buses or trains, and we had visions of riding southwards in rather more comfort and a great deal more quickly than we had managed hitherto.

When the time came for them to go I walked a little way down with them and she said:

'What a pity you can't come down now and have a bath and a change of clothes.'

'But I haven't brought my dinner jacket Eileen and anyway I should stink your flat out and you'd never get the straw out of the furniture. Bye!'

And I watched them walk down in the fading daylight to another farmhouse where they had left their bicycles.

They went back to Florence leaving us with the feeling that we were really in touch with people who might be able to help us, but very uncomfortable in my case because I had to hobble about in two left clogs until my boots came back. However, from this moment on things began to happen with great rapidity. Robin brought us a British Parachute Sergeant whom the Underground had spotted walking through the middle of Florence. He was a braw Scots laddie, with the bluest eyes you ever saw, ginger hair and freckles and not a word of Italian. He had walked hundreds of miles from a remote area in

Yugoslavia, often I guessed in circles and generally along main roads. I asked him what he wanted and he said 'A bicycle,' which we managed to procure for him through the good offices of Father Bonomi who also gave him advice and directions. Maddox observed:

'With the luck that chap's 'ad all along he'll ride straight through the front line and when he reaches an VIII Army unit I'll bet they'll be just brewing up a nice mug of char!'

Our boots were soon returned and with them I seem to remember Eileen had sent us some Epsom salts which may indicate what sort of condition we were in! I was also instructed to go to a house in Fiesole, the Villa Diana, the next day, where I would meet friends who would fix me up with false papers, transport etc. I went to the Villa Diana where photographs were taken for the identity cards and arrangements were made for us to be picked up in an ambulance on the Pontassieve side of Florence and conveyed on our way south. I was somewhat ill at ease in the well-dressed, elegant society in which I found myself and I was also rather concerned that so many people seemed to know who we were and what was afoot. But it did seem as though Eileen was doing the 'Gaoler's daughter' act in a rather big way. I recall very clearly that on leaving the Villa Diana I took my usual cross country route, ignoring the main gate and climbing over a wall, where I think that I may have been observed as I jumped down and walked away, and I have wondered ever since if this incident did not in some degree give the show away.

Anyway arrangements were made by a Doctor to pick up the remnants of the POWs in an ambulance near Pontassieve and we would ride on the next leg of our journey south. I hoped we would be able to follow up the POWs we had driven out of the Florence area and shepherd them a bit on their way. On 10th November six of us met a small ambulance as planned, we drove off in high spirits at having such swift and comfortable transport instead of footslogging over mountains and rivers. Our euphoria was short lived for around a bend in the road we met a posse of Carabinieri waiting in ambush and despite my protestations that we were highly infectious and suffering from dangerous diseases I was knocked down with the butt of a rifle and quickly shut up. We were ordered to empty our pockets into a blanket, and I lost my wallet, my money, my Camp Pay Book and the photographs of my wife and the daughter I had never seen. My ring and watch which I kept always in my socks and also my notebook and camp Diary which was inside my shirt I managed to keep.

I felt very bad about leading the other five into such a trap and was very worried about what might happen to Robin, Eileen, Father Bonomi and the others who had helped us in Florence. I also wondered if all the others I had persuaded to move on had been similarly snapped up, but there was nothing I could do about it and if there is nothing you can do about something there is no point in worrying. We were driven to a Parachute Battalion Barracks in Florence where we were deposited in a Barrack Room in front of the guard room.

The Barracks were surrounded by a high wall. Our room was bare and after a while a bowl of scalding stew was brought to us but, of course, we had nothing to eat it with except our fingers. We fashioned a spoon out of an old tin and managed to share it out somehow. I thought this would provide an excuse to make a protest, so I demanded to see the Commandante, who turned out to be a Kommandant. I can speak German but I addressed the Interpreter in English, and voiced my complaints, namely that I had been struck, we had been robbed of our possessions, no receipt had been given, there were no toilet or washing arrangements, we were not being treated in accordance with the Geneva Convention etc etc. To which he replied in German:

'Tell him there's a bloody war on, what does he expect me to do about it?'

The interpreter, obviously a diplomat, translated this as:

'The Commandant deeply regrets the treatment you have received and will enquire into this immediately.'

I continued:

'We have no cutlery or plates and all we have been given is a bowl of stew and we have nothing to eat it with.'

To which another rough, rude, soldier-like answer was returned to the effect that all good soldiers should always have a knife, fork and spoon and should know how to get over such piddling problems. This was again translated as:

'The Commandant regrets he has no stores and cannot supply your needs now but the matter will be looked into and rectified as soon as possible.'

I could scarcely keep a straight face and nearly answered the Kommandant in his own language and in his own way.

Having got nowhere with my visit to the Orderly Room, as an old lag, I set about looking for a chance to escape. Our room had a door which I found opened and there in the next room was a tray full of wire, pliers, etc which must have belonged to an electrician and, looking out of the window I saw there was a ladder, which he must have been using to repair wiring in the Barracks. This was leaning up against a hut some distance away. I took off my jacket, slung the tray round my neck, put a coil of wire over one shoulder and was about to walk out of the hut, pick up the ladder and find a quiet spot at which to climb over the wall when the look-out reported guards approaching. I threw down the tray and wire.

'Get up. Outside – you are leaving immediately.'

I put on my jacket and we were bundled into a lorry and taken to a railway station. Our numbers had been augmented by a number of Italian deserters and we were put in a queer Emmett-like, little third class compartment with a corridor down the left hand side and high backed seats over which you could see from one end to the other. There were the usual doors at each side of the carriage all of which had of course been locked.

In the station there were a few Italian officials and railway workers but they were kept away from us. One Italian girl from the Red Cross was allowed to approach the carriage and to her we gave our name, rank and home address etc and asked her to send news of our recapture to England, which she said she would try to do. In fact no news of our arrest ever reached England, which was just as well, because our families would have worried even more than before when no letters came from any German prison camp. We had now been at liberty for over two months and during that time we had had no means of sending any news to our families and of course we had received no news from home either. I think our families must have worried about us a great deal and the ex-prisoners, living in great uncertainty and privation, unable to understand Italian, missed the routine and regular meals of camp life and most of all they pined for letters from home. I cannot honestly say that I missed my letters to any great extent. I was too busy walking and talking my way through the mountains. I hoped that my family would not worry too much about me – after all the bad penny always turns up sooner or later. But I did hear that my mother put on a stone in weight when she got news that indicated that I had found sanctuary in the Vatican later on.

Eventually our carriage, after being shunted about, finished up in a large goods yard, where it waited until dark. There were soldiers or Carabinieri patrolling about and shots rang out periodically whether to discourage us from running away or thieves or partisans from attacking or robbing the railway we never knew. During this period I asked everyone if they wanted to escape or not and we laid our plans to jump off the train after it had left the station. Clearly everyone could not jump off the train and leave the guards alone to continue their journey, and of the private soldiers only one, a parachutist, wanted to make the attempt. Maddox and the others decided they had had enough of me and the mountains. Two young parachute officers and I completed the English contingent and two of the Italian officers decided to have a go as well. Our plan was to climb out of the rear carriage window and jump as soon as the train had left the suburbs of Florence. The British were to climb out of the left hand side windows and the Italians on the right. Those not jumping were to stand in the corridor so as to obstruct the view of the guards who had ensconced themselves in the front seats.

Four German soldiers, probably going home on leave, were to be our guards and I went and chatted to them and told them how much better it was to be in German hands again and how much we looked forward to being properly looked after in Germany, enquired after their families and so on and so forth. After a long time in the goods yard darkness fell and we guessed that the Allied Air Forces had probably deterred the Germans from moving military trains by day. At last we clanked out of Florence and soon cleared the town area, and with the powerful electric locomotive rapidly gathering speed we travelled westward on a high embankment across a flat plain, which must have been I think the Pian di Sco, brilliantly lit by an October full moon.

I decided the Paras should go first and show us how it should be done then the first two to jump should march up the line in the direction the train had gone and the last two march back to meet them. But the Paras said:

'No, it is going much too fast.'

So I climbed out of the window and down on to the bottom step and reaching up I clung to the old-fashioned brass grips by the door. By now the train was licking along and the ground close below my feet was rushing past at frightening speed. I couldn't jump and I couldn't stay in such an exposed and draughty position so I crawled backwards to the buffers where I hoped to be able to sit in shadow and out of the cold wind, but when I got there I saw to my horror that there above me was a sort of sentry box affair with a little window and a guttering light inside. It was occupied by a sentry who could see over the roof of our carriage along the whole length of the train and could give warning of air attack. Fortunately he didn't look down. Soon I was joined by the three other British parachutists and then an Italian appeared from the other side and was about to climb up to the sentry box, but I dragged him down just in time.

The engine started to freewheel and the lights of a station which may have been Sesto appeared ahead. We were on a high embankment, acacia trees grew on the steep sloping sides, and the whole scene was bathed in brilliant moonlight. We couldn't go through the station with five of us sitting on the buffers of the carriage and so as we gently slowed a little we jumped in the prescribed order. The two parachute officers, the private and then me. The Paras jumped and landed as they had been taught when coming down under a parachute. They rolled over and down the embankment. I went last of all, and never having been taught how to jump out of aeroplanes or trains, I jumped with my legs straight out in front of me hoping that my heels would hit the ground and my knees would absorb the forward momentum. I realise now that I should have rolled up in a ball, but I didn't and I went over flat on my chest in a flash and had all the breath knocked out of my body. I lay there completely winded and the long train rumbled by, its rear light flickered and grew smaller as I moved my hands, fingers and toes, arms and legs and discovered that, even if my back felt as if it was broken, my limbs were intact and I regained my breath. It was a marvellous moment and I smiled a great smile filled with emotion and relief at such an easy escape.

Our plan was that the first two would walk up the line and the last two would walk back and we would thus meet and make our way as quickly as possible back to Florence to give the alarm. I soon saw a tall rangy figure moving rapidly along the foot of the embankment and gave him a low whistle. It was the 1st Para officer. He hadn't seen No. 2 or the soldier. He helped me to my feet and we had to decide what to do. Of Para Officer No. 2 and the soldier nothing was to be seen or heard. Para No. 1 had walked up the line calling to his friends and seeking them but had found no trace. We concluded that they must have been knocked out or perhaps had wandered off in a daze. Para officer No. 2 we never saw again but the soldier turned up safe and sound the very next day.

I was eager to get back to Florence to warn our friends that we had been betrayed and anyway the main line from Florence to Germany was no place to hang around, so we crossed the tracks, scrambled down the embankment to the north and made our way over the little plain to the hills we could see in the moonlight.

The strip of plain which only looked a few hundred yards wide proved to be quite a formidable obstacle. There were wire fences to be negotiated and I, feeling that my backbone belonged to someone else, was not at my most agile. There were deep ditches full of water surmounted with wire and hedges, which took a deal of scrambling through, there was a little stream or river again guarded by wire to prevent beasts breaking through. We waded the stream, pushed and sloshed our way through the mud, reeds and rushes and clambered up the further bank and found ourselves at last on a road which ran along the foot of the hills. We walked a short way beside the road towards Florence in the black shade from the moonlight and then crossed it and set off upon a steep rocky track every stone of which showed white in the moonlight. As we stumbled upwards it seemed that every dog in every farmhouse started to bark, but nobody came out to investigate the cause of such a chorus.

Eventually, high up on the hill, to a crescendo of barking, we took shelter in a wood shed near a farmhouse from which we could dive quickly down the hill into a wood if need arose. The next morning we got a bowl of hot milky 'coffee' (the coffee in Italy was made with burnt bread or toasted acorns or anything which would turn the water black or brown) a crust of bread and we were on our way up and on towards Monte Morello. We were soon back on my old stamping ground from where I had carried out 'Operation Exodus' and we went to the lair of the band of partisans, who had just returned from a foray in the local town and there with them to our great surprise was our parachute soldier. Apparently he had been knocked out and when he came to all was quiet and nobody was about. He walked back in accordance with his instructions and went on walking until he came to what must have been some outlying suburb of Florence or a small village on the line through which we had run in the train. There, believe it or not, the first person he met was one of our partisan band who was engaged in a little local battle. They brought him back with them and we were reunited the very next day.

I soon learnt from the Pastores that the whole organization in Florence had been blown. The Villa Diana had been raided and everyone there had been arrested and taken off to prison including my Aunt Eileen. Robin, I was told, had escaped to Siena and the organisation lay in ruins. I later learnt that my Aunt was tried and sentenced to death. This was commuted by kind command of the Duce to 30 years imprisonment. She was liberated by partisans shortly before Florence fell about a year later. She tells me that Robin escaped, remaining at liberty in Siena and that after the war she went to Australia. In case she should happen to read this book, may I thank her for all she did for us and apologise to her and Eileen for all the trouble we caused them and to the Resistance organisation in Florence. From the ruin of our friends in Florence only those living in the hills outside remained.

The Parachutists went their own way having had quite enough of my company after all the trouble I had landed them in and the three South African officers, Ian McArdle, Sandy Stewart, Jack Seligman and I had to decide what we were going to do with ourselves. Of the South Africans, Ian McArdle was suffering from what sounded like tuberculosis and was too ill to undertake any further march. He was to be sistemato-ed* by the Fantonis and others and he remained in the Florence area successfully until the place was liberated a year later. When I last saw him he was living in Dunkeld near Johannesburg.

Sandy Stewart, Jack Seligman and I, having thought about the possibility of remaining in our cave on Monte Morello or joining a partisan band, decided we would continue to march south and try and get through to the Allies. On a cold day in November we walked for the last time over the hills to the north of Florence, said goodbye to our friends, the Paternas, Pratesis, Father Bonomi and others, and walked down those well-remembered paths, waded over the Arno river and started off towards Arezzo and Rome.

I had hoped that I would be able to persuade Eileen to give me her side of the story of what happened in Florence but she felt that for various reasons her tale should not be told. But she did not forbid me to tell her story and of course I was the cause of all her troubles and of those of the Villa Diana people. On 12th November she and most of the people in the Villa Diana were arrested, their property, houses, furniture and cars were seized and they were tried and sentenced to death for assisting us. Their sentences were commuted to long periods of imprisonment, in Eileen's case 30 years, and she remained in gaol until the Allies arrived in Florence. The Judge who commuted the sentences and the Director of Prisons seem to have been anti-Fascists at heart and Eileen was, I understand, given small tokens of encouragement during the period of her imprisonment which lasted for over a year. She was liberated by partisans shortly before the Allies entered

* Sistemato-ed, is to be looked after, hidden and protected.

Florence and was hiding in a house near the railway station when she saw two strange looking men creeping forward towards her. She soon saw that they carried kukris and recognised them as Gurkhas. The American V Army soon arrived and she cannot say enough about the kindness, generosity and consideration she received at their hands. She met General Mark Clark and eventually finished up helping our VIII Army in their further operations after the breaking of the Gothic Line which led to the advance into the Po Valley and the crossing of the River Po and indeed for the duration of all hostilities and the period of the occupation. Her fluent Italian, her knowledge of the country, its people and customs, were of inestimable value to the Allies.

I received this letter after my return to England:

Dear Major Darcy Mander,

We hope that you have reached the 8th Army in good health.

After you paid us a visit at Villa Diana, in Fiesole on November the 1st 1943 we also were victims of the spy who caused your capture while by car you were to reach the southern Italy.

We were afterwards informed that you courageously had been successful in escaping from the train, during the night which was to take you to Germany as a prisoner, since then we have had no news about you; but may be that was also due to our arrest which took place in the night of November the 12th 1943 and by the very group of nazifascist commanded by Major Carità of the SS of Florence.

Our story has been a very sad one for the weakness of some servant who once tortured confessed everything and also because of your little 'note-book' found in your possession at the moment you were captured and on which was signed by your own writing the address of Villa Diana, Elena Coutts Medici's name, our guest, the forged identity documents, the payment we had made you of 10,000, before these evidences we had nothing to obtest.

As a retaliation we were arrested and plundered of all our property, besides our cars and personal apparels, money and so on.

All is now confirmed by the proceeding made, at the time, by the Military Court of war of Florence and by the instructor Judge who for his antifascistic feelings cooperated with the director of the prisons of Florence to save us from the nazi-fascist's claws, who had sentenced us to death in accordance with a fascista decree of the 25th October 1943, for assistance to Allied prisoners.

We are now in possession of these documents and have submitted them to the Allied Screening Commission, to which we have applied, to obtain, on payment, a car in substitution of the three confiscated by the nazifascists at Villa Diana in the night of November the 12th 1943.

Since your declaration on the assistance we gave you would be of the utmost importance and would confirm our saying on the reason which caused our arrest, we would be obliged if you would send it to us in duplicate so that we can send one to the Allied Commission in Rome.

Your aunt Elena Coutts* is very well is on duty, actually, at Forli in a party of the 8th Army.

Hoping to hear from you very soon, accept our respectful greeting and our sincere sympathy.

Milan 29/8/1945   Fausta Gaston Zabban Belli
                                              via Cappuccini 14
                                                    Milano

I do not think my 'little note book' can have been evidence used against them because I still have the only note book I carried but I expect there may have been some piece of paper and the money which incriminated them. If I did carry a note book with names and addresses (I didn't know any addresses except the Villa Diana) I deserved to be shot.

---

* My Aunt's maiden name was Coutts. After the death of my uncle she married Signor de Medici and was in Benghazi until the Axis were driven out of North Africa.

VII

MARCH TO ROME

Today by way of the Autostrada the average Italian driver would, I suppose, allow a couple of hours to get from Florence to Rome. It is about 140 miles, so even a staid British motorist would not take very much longer. It took us about a fortnight during the latter part of November 1943 and we did the last 40 miles by train.

Sandy and Jack had both escaped from a Camp north of the Apennines. They too had been told to remain in their camp and the Germans had come along with talk of 'Armistice – now we can all go home' and carted nearly everyone off to Germany. They had got away and with Ian McArdle had made their way to Florence where Ian had remained. Now we three peculiar musketeers set out on the next stage of our journey south.

Both were from Johannesburg. Sandy Stewart, well over 6ft., looked rather like a fair youthful edition of Gary Cooper. When we got to Rome I made him walk in the gutter so that his height and his very English good looks should not be so apparent.

Jack Seligman was more my size and build. With his brown eyes and dark curly hair he could have passed for an Italian if he could just have got his tongue around the language. Later when in trains, buses, trams etc, if they wanted to talk they spoke in Afrikaans which effectively disguised their true identity.

They were both younger than me, and I was beginning to feel the effect of the jolt to my backbone and the accumulation of sleeping for nights on end in damp caves, barns and the like, for each morning when I got up I suffered from the most excruciating rheumatic pains, particularly in the legs, and I had to hobble after them until I had walked it off and got the blood circulating a bit.

We started out as we had done on our march to Florence, but, as we had been told, the country changed as we passed through Tuscany and the steep wooded hills and valleys gave way to wider, rounded hills with ever less cover. We still chose the most secluded lonely-looking route and avoided anything that remotely resembled a road but, due to the distance from which we could be seen, we walked well strung out.

I generally went in front and if I got involved with anyone the others would melt discreetly into the landscape.

Our plans were vague in the extreme. The general outline remained to continue to march towards our front line with the idea of crossing it, probably on the mountain tops where it would be lightly patrolled or else to pick up a boat and sail around the end of the line. After all Britannia did rule the sea and the air by now in this theatre of war so we hoped there might yet be a chance of a landing or something. If both ideas came to nought, and it was obvious that line-crossing would get very difficult as the winter wore on, then we would go to Rome and see what could be done from there. Clearly living in caves and barns in high remote areas throughout the winter was becoming a very unappetising prospect, and holing up in a wood for the night was by now out of the question. With these thoughts in mind we plodded through the Tuscan hills, like Hannibal without the elephants, past Arezzo, Perugia and Assissi, towards Terni and Rome.

On one particularly wet day in the neighbourhood of Arezzo we had been unable to find anywhere suitable to lodge. We plodded wearily along, wet, bedraggled, cold and hungry. Evening was upon us and in the fields among the woods there was no habitation visible, no sign of life or movement. The rutted track consisted of two rocky rivulets of muddy water and in the middle a stony path was only slightly less uneven than the ruts. Another little track joined ours, ascending from the valley on the right and in front at the entrance to a wood it divided left up the hill and right along the hill-side on which we seemed to have been walking since the dawn of time. We debated which path to take.

'I reckon that one to the left 'll lead somewhere fairly nearby. This damn track looks as if it goes all the way to Rome.'

'Might go to Orvieto or some village near there, but we don't want to go there anyway. Let's go a kilometre up there and if we don't come to anything we'll think again.'

We continued until at last we came to a large, quite prosperous-looking farm. It was not the sort of place we would have chosen, but it was reasonably isolated, so we decided to try our luck there. However, when I tried to talk my way in we were well and truly rebuffed and sent on our way. In our miserable condition such an event was very hard to bear, particularly after the universal kindness we had encountered further north in the Apennines. These people were farming on a much bigger scale. They had more to lose and didn't want to have anything to do with us.

The countryside ahead looked open and gently undulating – no hills or woods suggesting shelter or seclusion and we would obviously have to go some way in order to distance ourselves from the unfriendly reception we had received. There was nothing for it but to press on. How far we walked I do not know, perhaps it was only three or four miles, but tired, wet, hungry, cold and after the cruel repulse we had suffered at the last farm it seemed an eternity and a hopeless prospect, when at last we came upon another large farm similar to the last.

'Better luck this time.'

'Let us pray.'

Our reception, alas, was very similar. It was getting dark, it was raining, we were tired out and soaked through and I started talking as I had never talked before. Soon the poor farmer's wife was in tears.

'Let them in, I will talk to Luigi.'

Gratefully we entered the farmhouse and huddled over the fire while preparation for an evening meal went forward and I told them of our families far away and of our adventures as prisoners and at liberty in the mountains.

Suddenly the door opened and into the lighted room stepped a Corporal with the diamond-shaped fascist badge on his arm. His mother rushed at him and a torrent of Italian laced with gesticulation poured out over him.

'We couldn't turn them away. We had to let them in. Poor devils . . . wet . . . cold . . . starving. . .'

Luigi, overwhelmed by this emotional eloquence advanced to the fire side and we started to talk to him, he in his turn tried to turn his propaganda-fed arguments on us. He told the South Africans that they had been tricked into the war by the British and this fairly set them off. In their best 'infinitive' Italian they told Luigi they were volunteers, they would do it again, and that he was the one who had been tricked by the Germans; for once I could take a back seat and listen to my companions doing the talking. And very well they did it, for not only did we get a very good hot meal, but we slept in Luigi's bed, he slept in the barn. After all he was only a Corporal!

My memory of this part of our journey is one of lashing rain blowing horizontally across our path, muddy paths and leaky boots. We often spent the entire day soaking wet and there was no question of sleeping in the open in these conditions. Unfortunately, as Rosa and our many friends had forecast, the farms were bigger and more prosperous places than the primitive farmhouses where we had been so generously received in the mountains, and with the increase in size, numbers of people and prosperity, the warmth of our reception diminished to coolness or downright rejection and this made our progress even more difficult.

In the Regiment we have a picture of the 1st Bn The Green Howards fighting its way forward from Rome to the Gothic Line in the Apennines in 1944/45. It is a bleak, cold wintry scene with a few small figures dotted about a snow-covered landscape, warmed only by the flashes of exploding shells. I remember when it was presented to the Regiment one of the officers, Major O'Driscoll, examining the painting and, pointing to a rather tall figure, exclaiming:

'That's me!'

Well I was not featured in that painting but the scene was familiar and I realised I was looking at a landscape over which I too had passed.

'I have been there too', I said, 'but we were going in the opposite direction.'

Although so much was different I was forcibly reminded of our march in 1943 about a year before the events depicted in the picture took place. Instead of snow we had rain, instead of the scattered figures of the soldiers, there were just three tatterdermalion figures in a well spaced-out single file. Of course there was no shell fire, though we faced other hazards, and we had no tea, hot stew, good boots, warm clothing, letters from home or leave in Naples or Rome either.

The mud and the rain and the cold now became worse and we quite appreciated the difficulties the Allies were encountering as they tried to fight their way north from Naples that winter.

One day, as we were sloshing along over some wet fields, a lone ragged figure approached from the opposite direction. I said 'Buon giorno' as usual, received some muttered reply and passed by without a second thought when all of a sudden there was a shout:

'Marcus!'

'Jack!' and 'Good Lord, Sandy!'

It was Marcus Kane Berman a dental surgeon with the South African Army who had been in the same camp as the other two. He had attempted to cross the line, but had been re-captured, put in a cattle truck and shunted off by train to Germany. He managed to cut his way out of the truck and had decided to try and walk to Switzerland. He was in a far worse condition than we were and we soon fixed him up with some footwear and something to eat which so far as I could see he was just doing without.

In the company of his friends he soon decided, in the best traditions of Dick Whittington, to turn again and give it another go. He was a lively, amusing addition to the party, but he had grave news for us about the difficulty of getting through the lines. There was deep snow in the mountains and a wide zone had been completely cleared of all inhabitants behind the battle zone and he reckoned it was just about impossible anyway this winter. From the state of the going we had already experienced we did not need a lot of persuasion. Marcus for reasons of his own did not come with us to Rome. He was on his way to visit a place where he had stopped on his way south and I wondered if he had found someone like my Rosa.

As the going got worse, the mud deeper, the rain and wind more constant, so the state of our boots and clothing deteriorated correspondingly. Our Army boots had long since worn out and we wore an assortment of poor quality, ill-fitting footwear. At times I was reduced to wearing two left shoes or one clog and one boot and for these reasons and because of the very slow progress we made by our safety-first tactics, we started to take to the minor roads and thus began to meet all kinds of people we had never encountered before. Men in cars, lorry drivers, farm carts and tractors and Germans.

Apart from my brief acquaintance with the Kommandant and his guards in Florence, we had of course seen Germans on roads which lay in our path and in villages, but we had always successfully avoided meeting them up to now. Later on I was to get used to rubbing shoulders with them in Rome, and indeed I came to the conclusion that the closer I was to them, the safer I became because they would not think of looking for me under their very noses.

But at this stage of our journey it was a very different matter. One day we were walking along a narrow dirt road winding through the hills among groves of olive trees grown on the terraces hewn out of the hillside by the sweat of generations of Contadini. We were well strung out and I was in the lead when round a corner ahead came a German staff car followed by what looked like the beginning of a convoy of lorries, I shouted to Jack and Sandy and jumped down from the road into the olive terraces, which at that point turned out to be a drop of 12–15ft. Picking myself up I went leaping down from one narrow terrace to another until I was safely down away from the road and under cover. It was like a Hollywood film and we were, I suppose, the 'Baddies' being chased by the 'Goodies' – but we fervently hoped winning through in the end. In the film we would have made our escape with bullets kicking up the dust around our legs but we weren't chased. The convoy took no notice; it didn't stop, not a shot was fired and it motored serenely on its way. Dusting myself down I clambered back to the road and started to look for the others. Presently we were reunited and breathing heavily we resumed our way having resolved to keep a sharper look-out in the future.

Our next memorable encounter came on a wretched day, when we were resting in a shallow sandstone cave, reflecting cheerlessly on the plight in which we found ourselves. We were by now lousy and I had had to pick sheep ticks off myself – a legacy of an hour or two spent in a shepherd's yard where we watched Riccotta cheese being made from the sheep's milk and were given a good portion of it to eat, and warm milk to drink.

I suppose we had been spotted by some urchin for a figure appeared marching towards us. It was a woman. We stood up and she embraced us each in turn with a smacking kiss and, talking volubly all the while, led us to her habitation. She was a Communist, she was the first Communist I had ever knowingly met, she was certainly the first I had ever kissed! She opened our eyes to a whole new world of underground cell organisation which was to transform our lives in the immediate future. In no time at all she had all our clothes off our backs and we bathed in an open tin bath in front of a blazing fire. We scrubbed and shaved off all our hairs to get rid of the lice and she boiled our clothes and ironed them, particularly along the seams to burn out and destroy any remaining bugs or eggs. She also took charge of our onward journey and, although we did not know it, our days of wandering in the cold, wet wilderness were over.

One could say that our fate lay now in the hands of this splendid woman, who wore the trousers and ordered her meek, quiet, obedient husband about, but I think it would be truer to say that she took our fate by the scruff of its neck in her capable hands and decided what was to be done. We were to go to Soriano, and there the HQ would decide what would happen next. We said we wanted to get to Naples or if that was too difficult then Rome would be the next best thing.

'Of course,' she snorted, 'We can't keep you here or in Soriano for ever. And anyway it is stiff with Germans so you won't be there long.'

Her husband was sent off to warn the comrades and make preparations for our move and on his return many hours later he explained the plans he had made to which she vigorously agreed. We were to meet some comrades in a cave or wine cellar, cut into the side of the road leading to Soriano. There we would wait until dark when we would be escorted into Soriano where we would spend the night.

After the hot bath, with dried, de-loused clothes and a hot meal inside us we spent the night on the kitchen floor and, more cheerful, much happier and more confident, we set off the next morning for Soriano thanking our host and hostess most warmly for their help and hospitality. Matteo, a bright little lad, was detailed to act as our guide. He had his bicycle with him on which he was to ride home when he had delivered us to the wine cellar. He proudly pushed his sparkling machine along beside me or like the Pobble –

> 'He tinkledy binkledy winkled his bell
> as he peddled so slowly beside me.'

He chattered happily asking incessant questions about life in England, in prison, the war, everything. No silent Communist he! We, for our part clean and refreshed, dry, no longer crawling with lice and feeling better than we had for months, stepped out with a will, but again well strung out along the dirt road towards Soriano, which clung to a hill top like a gigantic limpet on an oversized rock some miles away to the west.

Suddenly a German army lorry was upon us and slowed to stop beside me and horror of horrors another came round the bend and yet a third, halted behind on the road ahead. No time to run, nowhere to run to either. Nothing to be done. No doubt it was a small convoy of supplies, perhaps taking rations, petrol, mail and ammunition to some AA battery or outlying unit. There were a number of soldiers on each truck, probably a guard.

I leant as casually as I could against the door throbbing with the steady beat of the engine, but hardly louder than my heart was beating. I reached up with my hands and curled my fingers as confidently as I could over the sill of the door and looked up at the driver and said 'Si?'

He looked down at my hands and to my dismay I saw that he was looking at my gold signet ring and I wished that it had been in my boot. However the motto inscribed on it, the family motto, is Italian anyway 'Vive bene' (Live well – a motto I had been very far from living up to recently).

At last he asked me the best way to get to Terni or somewhere or other, to which of course I had no idea of the answer so I directed him along the road we had just walked along, told him to turn right at a cross roads we had passed and fork left at an imaginary road junction some 4km down the road i.e., the first thing that came into my head and to my relief he revved up the engine, let in the clutch, thanked me warmly and shuddered away. I waved and the soldiers waved back. 'Buon viaggio.' 'Gracie!', they all disappeared down the road and I was alone.

I really was alone! Of Matteo there was no sign, nor did any amount of calling, whistling or searching produce a sign of him. I thought he had probably disassociated himself from us and pedalled on to Soriano or gone back home and told his mother that we had been arrested. It took me some time to find Sandy and Jack. They had walked quietly away, keeping going when they thought I had had it, I found them eventually discussing what should be done next and I joined in the debate. The day that had dawned so brightly had clouded over, hopes that had been so high, now tumbled quickly down into the depths of worrying doubt and uncertainty. We seemed to have slipped from the sure competent hands of our hostess, laundress and saviour of the night before and once more we were on our own.

We did what all good soldiers do in such a case – we appreciated the situation. The courses open to us seemed to be to return to our hosts of the night before, if we could find them, but this I was reluctant to do; to resume our march to Rome, which seemed to be presenting new difficulties as we went along; to head back into the mountains and try for the line, which we thought would be, to say the least, highly uncomfortable, unpleasant and probably impossible; or to carry on to Soriano and see if we could pick up Matteo or find the wine cellar, which sounded the more pleasant prospect, perhaps we would be picked up by comrades from the town on the lookout for us. We decided on this latter course.

Anxiously we set forth along the road towards Soriano. The fields became wider, the view more extensive, the cover less, and we felt very exposed. Of Matteo there was still no sign and he could not have been in the area because we could see for miles over that open empty rolling countryside. Presently to our left a rounded hill appeared and a tree-lined road ran along the side of it, obviously about to join our road a little way further ahead. The evening was drawing in and the light failing rapidly as we wondered which way to turn, when it occurred to me that there was a cutting on the far side of the road, in that cutting there might be some wine caves and in one of those caves . . .?

'Let's go and have a look.'

We turned left across the field in order to hit the road at the bottom of the hill where we walked along the verge in the dark shadow of the trees. As the hill rose before us there on the left hand side were a number of caves, each secured by a tall, rough wooden, padlocked gate, big enough to take a horse and cart. As we walked quietly along the grass verges we saw that one of the gates was open and the faint light of a guttering candle in the interior could be faintly discerned. We stopped, peered inside and saw the shadows of two or three men deep in the interior. They were the men who had been sent by our Communist to meet us, but had been told by Matteo that we would not be coming after all. They were just having a drink before shutting up shop and returning to Soriano. Another five minutes and we should have missed them. Of course they might have stayed tasting the wine from every vat buried deep in the bowels of the hillside and, if we had arrived an hour or two later we might have been guided to them by the sound of singing coming from the cave!

They greeted our arrival with great joy. Our Lazarus-like resurrection from what had been thought to be our German tomb, was enquired about, exclaimed over, and we might have been the cleverest fellows on earth instead of a scared trio who seemed to have their bad luck and good luck in very large but equal portions. We were pressed with a drink, and subjected to our usual nightly 'talk-in', during which we drank many a glass of good white wine, sampling many of the vats before any move was made to continue our journey. While they were used to taking wine, probably in large quantities every day, we were not and we had to watch our step with the drinking lest we were unable to do so when we got out in the cold night air outside.

At last the time came for us to go, and exclaiming:–

'They will be surprised to see you in Soriano'.

They put out the candle, chained up the door and we walked up the middle of the road in bright moonlight like any other group of six men who had been spending the last hour or two drinking in company. It must have been about 10 o'clock when we reached the cobbles and entered the town proper. We hadn't had anything to eat all day and the effects of the wine were wearing off. Soon the main square came into sight and it was jam-packed with people. The cinema had just finished and the audience was emptying into the square as we arrived. The audience were German soldiers.

I was perhaps getting a little more used to rubbing shoulders with Germans in uniform and that was exactly what we were doing as we pushed our way through the mêlee trying to keep up with our Italian companions. I had lived and studied in Germany before the war; and I could understand what they were saying so it wasn't so bad for me, but for Sandy and Jack it must have been alarming. The full moon was high in the sky and all faces and figures were clearly lit in even paler hue than no doubt our faces must have looked on account of the sudden unaccustomed proximity of the enemy. However the crowd soon dispersed and we made our way to a house seemingly built into the side of the hill, climbed some stairs and entered a civilised room with tables, chairs, pictures and books on the wall. There were electric lights with shades, rugs on the floor and we were invited to sit down in comfortable chairs and have a drink. What a change from the rough farm houses we had been previously accustomed to!

Our host was a tall, well-educated man. I think perhaps he was a Doctor, Professor or teacher and he and his wife made us feel quickly at home. But it was to the daughter that our eyes were 'involuntarily' drawn. She was the most delightful girl you could possibly imagine, and her already animated expression was heightened by the excitement of talking to three Allied officers under her own roof, the more especially since we had been reported as having been captured that very day. Again we had to recount the day's adventures, which under such bright brown eyes no doubt lost nothing in the telling.

We were ravenous and tucked into sausages with gusto when they were put on the table. Suddenly I stopped eating;

'Is anything the matter?'

'Surely these are German sausages?'

Everybody laughed and Liza blushed to the roots of her hair.

'Yes, they are German Army rations. Liza gets them from her German boy friend. You will meet him directly.'

When the implication of this laughing reply sank in, I was somewhat concerned.

'Is this really wise?'

When it was explained to Jack and Sandy they nearly jumped out of the window.

'Oh no! It is quite alright! He is a real friend of the family. He wants to desert to the British Army actually!'

'Good God you don't expect us to take him with us do you?'

'Of course not but after you get to Rome perhaps he might run away and join you there.'

Soon in through the door walked a very large, well-fed German Corporal wearing the badges of a signal unit. He addressed Liza and her parents in Italian and turned to us and spoke to us in excellent English. His name was Hans.

I complimented him on the sausages.

'Yes,' he said, 'they are very good, they are Luftwaffe sausages.'

'Flown from Germany daily I suppose,' I replied, and the atmosphere, which had been rather electric, relaxed and became a little easier.

It appeared that Hans was working in a wireless interception unit which besides signallers and wireless experts was staffed with linguists, code breakers, mathematicians and other boffin-types, who did not always make the best Nazis. We gathered that most of the intellectuals, of whom he was one, knew from their work what the true situation was, and reckoned that Germany had already lost the war. We settled down to a pleasant evening's conversation, which was only broken up by the necessity for us to get some sleep and for him to be back in camp for roll call.

When I got to Rome and had established communications with our side I reported the existence of this intercept unit, but I think our people already knew all about it and were probably making use of it, because I never heard that our Air Forces ever paid Soriano a visit. Later on Hans did indeed desert and to my horror, dressed in civilian clothes, he sought me out in Rome and asked for my help. I thought I was already imposing on my friends in Rome sufficiently and could not possibly wish a German Corporal on to them, but we tried to get him into the Vatican by way of a coal hole while coke was being delivered to the Papal boilers.

After the war he was arrested in Italy and sentenced to a long term of imprisonment for what crimes I have no idea. I wrote to the British Military Government in Soriano and tried to explain the case, but I never heard if my representations had any effect. I fear that our authorities may not have believed a word of it.

VIII

ARRIVAL IN ROME

After the excitements of the day and the rapid changes in our fortune we slept, but fitfully, although we were in real clean beds with clean sheets, a luxury we had not known for a long time.

We were to make an early start for Rome next day, a distance of about 30 or 40 miles, by train. This worried Jack and Sandy, but we were assured that all would be well, two friends would travel with us, get the tickets and hand us over to the 'Organisation' in Rome.

'Don't worry Sandy, it is better than walking.'

But Sandy did worry. After a very early and hurried breakfast we said a warm goodbye to our hosts, promising to look after Hans if he ever did get to Rome. We went to the station as dawn was breaking and joined a throng of people on the platform jostling each other and chattering loudly as is the habit of Italians in a crowd. Our tickets had already been bought for us and when the train arrived we fought our way on board, standing in the corridor as the train was already over-crowded when it arrived.

For myself I was pleased and happy, almost exultant – like Mr. Toad, I felt like saying 'This is the way to travel! No more mud, no more walking! Poop Poop – the only life.' Knowing my propensity for getting into trouble you may wonder if a disaster similar to that which landed Mr. Toad in the canal was not now about to strike, and you would be quite right. We landed in our canal that very day and the water was as cold and inhospitable as Mr. Toad's. But for the moment nothing more serious than Sandy fainting for lack of air in the corridor happened.

'Povero – open the window – give him air!'

'Gracie. Gracie.'

The crisis was over though Sandy remained very pale and apprehensive until the end of our journey. We arrived in due course at our station in Rome which was semi-underground rather like the District Line in London. The train disgorged its passengers, us with them, we shuffled slowly along the platform and there in front of us at the ticket barrier were two armed Carabinieri.

'Waiting for us,' breathed Jack into my ear.

What a terrible thing is a guilty conscience. We walked past them with no trouble at all out of the forecourt into a small Roman square. The pale winter sun was shining, the Contadini were freshening up their vegetables in a horse trough, and there were shops and cafes. People were walking about quite normally and our friends went off to make contact with their Roman comrades.

We had arrived and done so safely! It was a lovely day; we were in the hands of friends; we had achieved our immediate object, and anyone else would have thought that this was a happy day, an occasion for rejoicing, something to celebrate. If you thought that you would be quite wrong. There we sat, three Allied officers dressed in the most fearful mixture of clothing, not knowing a solitary soul in the whole of Rome, with hardly two pennies to rub together. We felt very conspicuous, our friends had gone, we knew not where, to arrange for our reception, which evidently was no easy task for they were away a very long time, most of the day in fact. We began to wonder if we should ever see them again and what on earth we should do as strangers in the enemy capital, when at last they returned and told us that we were to go with them to a flat where we would spend the night.

They took us across Rome by tram changing en route, arriving in a working class district of Rome where building sites outnumbered the completed buildings. We were taken to a large block of flats, entering by the back entrance, where we were shown to the Portiere's flat, which was small and warm. Our friends departed and the Portiere made a short speech. He said that we should never have been brought to Rome, that we could stay only one night and would then have to find other accommodation. We could sleep in an empty flat at the top of the building, but we must make no noise or the people in the flat below would hear. Chastened by this reception – so different from that of the day before – we took off our boots, went silently up the back stairs and at the very top of the building we were admitted to the empty flat. There was no furniture, light or heat and the floor was tiled, cold and hard. We were once again enjoined to be very quiet as nobody was supposed to be there at all. I asked for some newspaper to put on the floor to sleep on and this and a light meal was all we had from the Portiere.

Our fortunes had once again nose-dived and we were close to despair. I had no idea how we were to set about finding ourselves anywhere to stay in Rome the next day. We discussed our dilemma in low anxious whispers and decided that next morning I would go to the Swiss Embassy, which was the office of the Protecting Power, and see what could be done.

Next morning we got some coffee and bread from the Portiere and, warned again that we must be out of the flat by nightfall, I went down to his flat and asked to borrow the telephone directory. I looked up the Swiss Embassy, wrote down the address and asked my host how to get to that part of Rome. I was told what tram to take, where to change trams and I set off without much hope of achieving anything and knowing there was no hope of persuading the Portiere to keep us in that awful flat even if we could stick it much longer. Although I had not been in any town for some years and the past few months had been spent avoiding even villages and I had never been to Rome before, I managed to find my way about Rome reasonably well. Rome is a difficult place to get your bearings in; its seven hills are easily confused and the city has no cohesive shape. It seemed very large and extensive after Soriano and our previous wanderings in the Italian countryside, but I found the Swiss Embassy quite easily and marched through the front door in the Via Veneto and asked to see Captain Trippi, who had visited our camp during our imprisonment, his being the only name I knew in Rome save that of the Pope. I was told to wait and sat down on a bench on which there was already an occupant, who sat there silently with a small boy. I hoped he would not have business with the Captain and that if he did it would not be of long duration when I began to wonder:

'He doesn't look very Italian. Could he possibly . . .?'
I turned to him and said very quietly in English:

'You aren't British I suppose are you?'
He was Tug Wilson and had already been in Rome for some time and, although pretty well 'sistemato-ed', was busy trying to improve his situation. I poured out my story to him and he said he knew just the chap.

'Give me ten minutes with Trippi and we'll go and meet him.'
Tug went all over Rome with the small boy who bought tram tickets, acted as a guide and interpreter and was most useful, as I shall explain later. Soon we were off to the Vatican and there, near the grand collonade outside we met Franko.

Franko – real name Branko – was a Jew who was a travelling actor, dancer, acrobat or circus performer from the German-speaking part of Yugoslavia. He and his wife had been imprisoned by the Fascists and he had escaped at the time of the Armistice and had come to Rome to carry the fight to the enemy by any means in his power. Assisting POWs was one of his activities. As a Jew he was not very well received in the Vatican and he suffered from another handicap: his Italian was negligible and nobody in Rome could understand Serbo-Croat or whatever language it was he spoke. The only western language he could speak was German and that was not very popular in Rome either. He was getting very frustrated very fast when I appeared on the scene. As a British officer who spoke German and who could promote his plans with the Vatican and other Allied organisations, I was a gift from the Gods. We repaired to a cafe where we drank some cognac and had a coffee. Tug left us with, needless to say, my warmest thanks ringing in his ears.

'When shall we meet again?'

'Oh, don't worry, we will. One bumps into chaps in Rome in the most surprising way. Franko knows where I live – he found me the flat.'

As soon as Tug Wilson had departed I urged upon Franko the need for haste but he was in no hurry. He was, I suppose, satisfying himself that I wasn't a German stool-pigeon planted among the POWs and I think my German was a good deal better than his so I might well have excited some suspicion on this count. The next thing he did was to take me to a shop and buy me a hat.

'Sie brauchen einen anständigen Hut, mein Lieber.' (You need a good hat, my friend.) And I must say it improved my appearance a lot. At last I got him to the trams and we reached the block of flats only late in the afternoon. I thought it advisable not to introduce him to the Portiere but left him at a corner cafe, went to the Portiere and up the stairs two at a time to poor Sandy and Jack.

'Where have you been?'

'We thought we'd had it.'

'He's been up here three times telling us we've got to get out.'
They were sick with worry and I had no time to reassure them with words.

'Come on – tell you later. We've got somewhere. Come on – quick.'
We crept down the back stairs, said a brief and a silent farewell to the Portiere and went to the tram stop. Thus it was that within 48 hours, the Communist party, which had welcomed us with kisses in the country, spewed us coldly out after only a night and a day in their hands in Rome. But there was no time for such thoughts. I was delighted with our progress. From the very depths of the night before

we were apparently on the crest of a wave once more. We had weathered yet another storm, surely nothing would sink us now. And true enough nothing ever did sink me, but many of my friends were not so lucky.

Franko saw me and sauntered over without a word and without acknowledging my presence, and I too ignored him. I was learning fast. Once we were on the tram and on our way he joined us and we chatted in German, which wasn't very reassuring for Jack and Sandy and I told them as much as I could of Franko, although at this stage I had only known him an hour or two – how I had met him, about Tug and his flat and about our destination – another flat where the Portiere was a bit more accommodating than our friend of the night before.

Changing trams in the middle of Rome, we went by trolley-bus to a residential quarter where tree-lined streets of substantial villas greeted our eyes.

'More like it, Sandy, isn't it?'
Sandy raised a faint smile and told me by his expression to shut up and not to draw attention to myself. We got out of the trolley-bus and walked a few blocks through side streets until we arrived in the Via D.Chelini where we entered a large palatial block of flats via the garage entrance. We found ourselves in the basement of a large mezzanine floor flat which gave on to the Via D.Chelini and was, I suppose, officially shut up. Inside the flat there were about 8 or 9 prisoners of war, mostly officers, mostly British, and there they lived shut up from the outside world with nowhere else to go. How the flat came to be put at our disposal in the first place will be related later. Whether anybody paid for its use I doubt, but the priests from the Vatican fed us. One of the English priests came regularly with a great basket of rolls and other items of food, which was cooked by a Jewish girl, also a refugee, who had been installed to look after us.

Franko was well known to them all and was delighted that at last he could talk to them through me. They on the other hand may well have suspected that I was a German and not British at all, but Jack and Sandy vouched for me and I was accepted. Later on, however, when the flat had been raided in my absence and I was the only one to escape, the story that I was some sort of dangerous double agent went around Rome and many a door was slammed in my face when I was in need of help or shelter.

Now began a new kind of life altogether. Franko, of course, went all over Rome as free as a bird and I too had no idea of being cooped up in some form of voluntary self-immurement that seemed to me worse than prison. I went to see Captain Trippi who told me where to get Red Cross parcels. I took Jack and Sandy around a bit, with Sandy walking in the gutter as I mentioned before, and got them Red Cross parcels too. It seemed an odd thing to do and we didn't make a habit of it as we thought the place might well be watched, we could be followed on our way home with the loot, and anyway they were not very happy walking about the city or travelling in trams and buses.

Although we were very grateful for our shelter we were by no means convinced that so many of us could live undetected and undenounced to the enemy when a large bounty was payable for each POW betrayed to the Germans. So we told Franko we would like a smaller place where we three could live rather more safely and discreetly than the crowd in the Via D.Chelini.

This crowd had a tendency to increase steadily. A Doctor arrived one day, closely followed by a private soldier who had lost his mind. Soon after our arrival, who should walk in but Marcus Kane-Berman who had been picked up by the grape-vine and brought unerringly back to us. He was ribbed a bit about the supposed coldness of his Italian girl-friend but he was in very much better shape than when we left him so his friends, whoever they or whoever she was, had done a lot for him. Our numbers were now seventeen and there seemed to be an awful lot of people who knew all about our flat and also two other flats, one of which housed mainly Warrant Officers and NCOs and the other one, private soldiers. Many of those in the know were from the Vatican but did not need to know, and, although an excellent institution in things spiritual, the Vatican certainly seemed to lack the security and discipline which needed to be MI5-like and a bit more in the circumstances in which we lived. Although in fairness to the Vatican boys I must say that the raid on the Vatican flats was entirely our fault. With seventeen officers in the flat we urged Franko to hurry up and find us something else. I for my part redoubled my efforts to expand my circle of friends so that I had sufficient safe houses to which we could go if we had to move out in a hurry.

The very first people I was introduced to by Franko were Lodzi and Nora Kiss (pronounced Kish – it is the equivalent of Smith in England) and Daniele. I took Jack and Sandy to Nora's flat during the time we were in the Via D.Chelini flat and I am sure the visit did them a lot of good. Nora was a splendid person. She was Russian and was born in a summer resort near Baku. Her parents were well-to-do gentle-folk and she was a young girl when the revolution started in 1917. Her parents invited the peasantry and the revolutionaries to their house and tried to 'educate' them a little. Nora's father played the piano and entertained their guests, who moved in on them pretty rapidly and soon Nora and her mother fled in a sleigh, pursued by wolves and Bolshevik guards, and finally arrived in Paris leaving her father, who was a gentle soul, to make a living playing the piano or as best he could.

Mother and daughter settled in Paris and Nora studied dancing. I remember Paris as a young man in the twenties when I was in my teens, and it was full of simply gorgeous young Russian girls, all of them seemingly princesses and most of them penniless. But to the best of my recollection they did not remain so for long. Nora became a ballerina and eventually married Laszlo Kiss, a Hungarian actor turned film producer. I will call him Lodzi, because that seemed to be the way his name was pronounced. Lodzi was making films in Rome when war broke out and they were still there when France was overrun and they thought that to go back to Paris would be leaving a bearable frying pan to see if the fire was more comfortable. The film-making came to an end as the war went on, but Nora carried on teaching dancing in Rome and Lodzi scratched a living as best he could as an alien in Fascist Italy.

Nora was small and dark with black hair and large black eyes. She was imperious by nature and did not suffer fools gladly. She could shout and stamp her foot in the studio where she taught dancing and she could do it in her home too if she became impatient at the stupidity or slowness of those to whom she was talking. She was highly intelligent, spoke Russian, perfect French, very good English, Italian and also German. Lodzi was very good-looking and easy going, although as a Hungarian he had great difficulty in wrapping his tongue round foreign languages. He spoke French, English, Italian and German well, but with a pronounced accent.

Nora taught most of the cabaret dancers in Rome at a studio not far from her flat, which incidentally was not far from the Via Tasso torture chambers of the Gestapo. Her students were a marvellous bunch of boys and girls. They had very little money and often paid her with eggs or a chicken or something obtained on the black market, or possibly from the Germans they entertained at their work in the cabarets. I remember Nora tried me out in her flat and told me that I would make a dancer, but may be I was not good-looking enough or too bow-legged and anyway by then I had too many other fish to fry and had no desire to spend hours a day being yelled at by her in her studio, although it would have made very good cover.

Nora was immensely proud of her Russian homeland and, at this stage of the war, it was the Russian armies that were scoring great victories and advancing in giant strides westwards towards Europe whilst we were seemingly stuck fast at Cassino. The Kiss's were as thick as thieves with the Communists and all the many other underground groups in Rome although, here perhaps I should make the point that they didn't actually like the Communists any more than I did, but they worked with them perforce because they were the only organised resistance movement in Italy at this time. From them I was given much good advice, which enabled me to make an excellent start in Rome.

Nora had left Paris in the winter of 1939–40 to join Lodzi in Rome and shortly after her arrival a complete stranger thrust a piece of paper into her hand and hurried away. Thinking it was some clandestine matter she walked home and only in the privacy of her flat did she open the paper and read the contents. This is what she read.

The Prophecy of St Odile
   'There will be a terrible war, which will be started by a man born on the Danube. In the first part he will win all the battles very quickly and no one will be able to stop him. In the second part the battles will go this way and that way and the third part will be short and will start after the battle reaches the Holy City.'

At that time the Germans had occupied Austria and Czechoslovakia and were facing the Russian Armies in the middle of Poland. Later when the German armies had reached her native Caucasus and stood at the gates of Alexandria, Nora wondered how the war would end quickly if it was approaching Jerusalem, but as she drank her very last cup of tea on the balcony of her flat and saw the fighting going on in the hills around Rome in June 1944 and heard the news of the Allied landings in Normandy she remembered the prophecy.

St Odile was born blind, cast out by her family and adopted by a Convent, where she miraculously regained her sight. She became Abbess and foundress of Hohenburg now Odilienberg and her life abounds in extraordinary legends. She died in A.D. 720. I have since learnt that the prophecy was bogus; but that a phoney prophet of 1939/40 did forecast the end of the war in 1945 in a remarkable way.

Daniele was a young Italian who was called up and sent to the Russian front. There he was captured and put to work by the Russians. He spoke fluent Russian and he must have been able to persuade the Russians that he was a good Communist for he was given his freedom in Russia to such an extent that he married a Russian girl whilst a 'prisoner' in Russia.

Whether he was sent to Italy by the Russians to form a cell in Rome or whether he escaped from Russia and returned by devious means, I do not know, but he had returned to Rome by 1943, bringing his Russian wife with him. I remember that I had a meal in their flat on my birthday on the 11 December 1943 and I produced some items of food from a Red Cross parcel one of which was a portion of plum pudding. Daniele's wife could not speak English or Italian, so I never was able to get to know her well. Here perhaps I should mention that whereas in this story I have used the real names of the people who walked upon my little stage, in Daniele's case I have not done so for reasons which will appear later.

And now I must get back to telling the story of what went on in the Via D.Chelini flat in Rome in December 1943 – January 1944. I think that there must have been a Jonah-like quality about me during this period of my life. Although I do not think I was directly or even principally responsible for the disaster in Florence, I expect that I was, if not the direct cause, at least as blameworthy as anybody else for the fate of our friends in that area. Here in Rome I had taken a leading part in ensuring security, keeping all windows shuttered, keeping the inmates out of sight when anyone came in, bell signals, alarm drills, and so on, and yet again I was directly instrumental in provoking the blow which duly brought down our house of cards.

Franko had found us another flat à la Tug Wilson and we were to move out the next day. He produced a porter because we had accumulated quite a lot of gear and we did not wish to be seen going in to our new abode obviously equipped for a long stay and carrying suitcases. When I returned to the Via D.Chelini flat that day I found the porter in the room with all seventeen officers. I was very annoyed. It was against all the rules and quite unnecessary. There was the front room or the hall in which one or two of us could have talked to him if this was necessary without his knowing that anyone else was in the flat. I remonstrated sharply with Franko in German.

'Oh, he's alright, he's done jobs for me at both the other flats.'

'What? He knows about all three?'

I was horrified. However we were leaving next day – thank God – and we would probably move again or devise some sort of 'cut-off' from this organisation where far too many people seemed to know far too much.

We spent a happy evening preparing for our departure the next day. Franko would get the place ready and lay in some food in the morning, we would move in during the afternoon and the porter would come for our luggage later. But the porter came at midday the next day, and there were German soldiers with him and they took the men and left the luggage.

The next morning I set out bright and early on my usual forage around. I had a lot to do and wanted to be back early on account of the move. First of all, I wanted to get hold of some money and, since we would no longer be fed by the priests from the Vatican, do something about getting hold of some food. I had some success in regard to the money and I had also managed to get in touch with someone who would provide me with ration cards. Franko was going to stake us out on our arrival and I hoped that in a day or two we would be able to manage.

It must have been about 3.30 p.m. on a fine afternoon in early January that I walked down the Via D.Chelini. There were some people about so I walked past our flat and waited for the coast to clear before going in. I ran cheerfully up the broad front steps, no one in the hall, turned to my left and gave the signal on the bell. The door opened. I noted with approval that my strictures about security had been observed to the letter, nobody was visible in the sitting room. Nobody was visible because nobody was there except for two figures in uniform in the hall one of whom held a rifle pointed at my stomach and the other, who said in German: 'What do you want?'

I would like to say that I put on an act, and pretended to be frightened, but let us say that it wasn't very difficult! I stammered something in Italian about 'coming to fetch some documents.' (Actually I was translating a play into English and incidentally found the Pinero-esque jokes and humour peculiarly difficult to put into light-hearted slangy English in such surroundings.) So I went to my room – there were all my things ready – pretended to rummage about and produced the play and exclaimed:

'Ah, there it is!' and turned beaming at the guards who only replied:

'Wait here until the Capitano arrives.'

'That's torn it,' I thought 'An Italian. I won't get away with it with an Italian.'

You can imagine my thoughts. I had no idea what had happened to

Jack, Sandy and Franko or what had gone wrong and I could think of no convincing tale to tell the Capitano when he arrived. I had no identity document and my Italian was far from perfect. It looked very much as if I had had it and would be joining my friends in whatever black hole it was they had got into.

The soldiers indicated a bench in the unfurnished front room which led from the hall through an archway and the shutters of which were, like the others, kept permanently closed as these windows gave onto the Via D.Chelini, and told me to wait there. They sat on a bench in the hall waiting like spiders for any further flies that might walk into their trap, and it so happened that there was in fact another fly outside. They were out of my sight but I could hear them talking quietly in the hall. I crept mouse-like to the window, slowly pulled the shutter strap and silently lifted the shutter a little. There, looking up at me from the pavement below was Cesare Coen, the fiancé of our nice Jewish girl who had lived in the basement part of the flat and who had cooked, washed and mended for us there. I put my finger to my lips, enjoining silence, threw my briefcase down to him, put my legs across to the sill like a high jumper on the bar and dropped down to the pavement about 10–12ft. below and ran. There was no pursuit, no shots, all was quiet. My absence had not been spotted, and I am sure, that when the Capitano arrived, the guards agreed to say that nobody had called at the flat rather than admit that anyone had got away.

Round the first corner we slowed to a rapid walk and I told Cesare what had happened and I tried to think what to do. Here I was in yet another scrape and I was soon to learn that I was in an even stickier mess than I had at first conceived. I was once more on my beam-ends. I had lost my bed, board and lodging also my clothes, shaving gear and all my possessions. I had lost my friends and also Franko who had been our main support in Rome and, apart from the food from the Vatican and from the Red Cross, had also been our main provider.

I had been around quite a lot in Rome and had a wide circle of friends. A British Army officer, who wandered about freely and openly in Rome and who spoke Italian, was a very popular chap and much in demand. I had friends in all walks of life and all parts of Rome, from counts and countesses, priests, professors, Russians, Danes and cabaret dancers to thieves and black marketeers. In such a desperate situation I turned immediately to Nora.

Nora's flat was close at hand and Nora was the very person to go to when in trouble. As it turned out, it was a very good thing I went directly there, but I made a big mistake in taking Cesare with me. If I had had time to think I would have told him to go home and gone to Nora alone, and Cesare must have been badly shattered by the news I had given him or he would not have gone with me just before the curfew but would have gone straight home.

Running and walking as fast as we could I told Cesare as much as I knew of what had happened. As we entered the block of flats in the Piazza Fiume where Nora lived, we were greeted by the Portiere whose responsibility it was to account for the presence of strangers in the building. We rushed up the stairs to the top floor and no doubt incoherently gave Nora an account of the day's events. It was now curfew and everybody had to be home by then. Doors were shut, streets were empty, we were trapped.

Nora did some rapid telephoning: 'Daniele?' And there followed a rapid conversation in Russian. In about a quarter of an hour a car drove up and a few moments later into the flat, in the full splendour of an SS uniform, strode Daniele. I gasped. I knew him perfectly well. I was about to exclaim. . . . Nora put her hand on my arm. She had not explained the situation to me because of the presence of Cesare and because of the complexity of the matter. Nora spoke rapidly and at some length to Daniele again in Russian. He looked pale and alarmed. But finally he drove off into the night with Cesare and left me with Lodzi and Nora and I was soon to learn the depths of the disaster in which we found ourselves.

Now my tale becomes rather complicated and you may think improbable, but I assure you that it is true. The Via D.Chelini flat was known to us as a Vatican flat and we had received food from the priests daily. But now we enter a world of agents, double agents, double-cross and triple-cross and I will try and make the position as clear as I can.

The flat had been owned by people who had been arrested either by the Gestapo or the Italian equivalent. The Gestapo or whatever the German Security Service in Italy was called, employed a number of Italians and one of these was Daniele. He knew about the flat and had taken part in the raid on it and in the arrest of the occupants and had the key. Since it was empty and unused, he thought it would make a very good safe house and so he handed it over to us POWs. Daniele was a double agent and of course the Germans didn't know what he had done.

Soon after getting back to Rome he was involved in some street fracas and was arrested, but somehow he was bailed out by his father who was a Colonel in the Italian Army, and through whose good offices he was offered a post in the German SS.

Daniele had approached Nora in the first place so that his wife, who spoke no Italian or any other European language, could have someone to talk to in Russian, but Nora had little time for her because she seemed to be neither fish nor fowl nor good red communist herring. But Daniele had a great respect for Nora and when he was offered this appointment he went and asked her if he should accept it.

It was obvious that there were tremendous advantages in having someone in the SS in Rome and I would have jumped at it right away and told him to accept but Nora, who knew him much better than I did, said she would think it over and let him know. In the end they decided to advise him to accept, provided he told them what was going on and what was going to happen at the SS HQ, which he agreed to do.

I suspect that he pretended to be a Communist in Russia, but I don't think he was ever a committed one and he certainly was not one of the Stalin worshipping Italian crowd. Neither was he a Fascist like his father, and it became quite obvious that he wasn't on our side either. I came to the conclusion that he worked for himself and nobody else. To the Communists he was a Communist, to the Fascists he was Fascist and to us he acted the part of a Fascist and we got a great deal of benefit from that. As an Italian employed by the SS he was mainly employed on security work and I never got any military information from him, but we were able to warn people of raids and arrests. He was also instrumental in saving a number of Jews from arrest and deportation to somewhere like Treblinka or Auschwitz, but strangely there were cases where he could have saved them but did not do so. Perhaps there were rich pickings to be had in these cases and he wanted the money. On one occasion we made use of him to get Lodzi out of gaol. Lodzi had been caught trying to sell gold on the black market and was in the hands of the Italian Police. We told Daniele to go and tell them that the Germans wanted him and get him out, which he did, to the fury of the Italians. He also got the gold, but he only handed over Lodzi to us.

I do not know what happened to him after I left Rome, but I know he had the idea of going to South America. Many Germans were sending money there via Egypt and Spain and I expect he was doing so as well. Since there were a lot of German and Austrian Jewish refugees already in South America, who were joined by Nazi Germans fleeing from retribution after the war, perhaps Daniele was able to continue his little game, being all things to all men and being true to no one but himself.

When the news got around that twenty or thirty POWs had been arrested in that flat you will realise that Daniele would have some explaining to do. Nora realised at once that his goose would be well and truly cooked. The Germans would want to know why those British officers were in that flat and the Vatican and the Underground would no doubt think that someone had betrayed them and would suspect him. So would the Communists and it must have seemed to anyone except Nora that he was blown so badly that there could be nothing for it but for him to disappear. But Nora had already worked out a plan for such a contingency and she told Daniele what had happened and what he was to do in Russian so that Cesare should not know what was afoot.

When Daniele had taken Cesare home she sent Lodzi down to square the Portiere and so permit me to stay in the flat that night. Upon Lodzi's return we all had a stiff drink and they explained the story of the flat to me, and also told me what she had told Daniele to say and do when the news broke at the German Security HQ that there were twenty POWs in his flat – and this is what Nora told him in Russian that afternoon.

'When you are told about the raid you must pretend to be utterly astonished and very angry and say that you had carefully arranged for the prisoners to be in the flat because a Very Important Russian General (VIRG) for short was expected in Rome shortly and that you hoped to catch him there. The whole plan was ruined. (You could then demand that the prisoners should be sent back there, and if not all, anyway at least two or three – Sandy, Jack and Marcus – and it might not be too late to get the VIRG.) How can I work if you are so hamfisted and have sprung my trap just when it was all set?'

And do you know, it worked. Or it would have worked if there had not been a scare about an Allied landing and, as a consequence, all POWs in the Rome area were whisked away smartly to the north. I do not know what sort of a job Daniele had before he was called up but I reckon he must be an actor of Hollywood star quality to get away with a story like that with a lot of hard-faced Germans. But Daniele's cover was preserved and he and his wife went to live in the flat, ostensibly to catch the VIRG and I stayed there sometimes because I reckoned that as a twice-raided flat occupied by an SS man, it must be just about the safest spot in Rome. And of course I got my underwear back.

But I fear I am getting rather ahead of events. Up to that moment I knew nothing of these things. I thought of the flat as a Vatican flat and whilst Lodzi went down and told the Portiere that I was a German Officer, Nora cooked us some supper and in the process, was no doubt cooking up further refinements to add to the tangled web she had already woven. On his return Lodzi explained it all to me and told me of this hare-brained idea of what Daniele was to say to the Germans. We talked far into the night. I wondered how I would manage in this new world with a betrayed spy in the Gestapo, no flat, no food, and no Franko and I spent the night on the tiled floor, which was only slightly less hard and cold than the floor on which we had slept on our first night in Rome. My thoughts and dreams were as troubled as they were on that occasion, since it seemed that I had once again got into a fearful pickle and had yet again reached the bottom of my fortunes.

The next day however there was work to be done. Nora and Lodzi had to tell the Underground and the Communists about the Via D.Chelini raid and I had to tell the Vatican organisaion what had happened. Bad news travels fast however, and in the murky underground waters of Rome it travelled very fast indeed. When I went to see Mons. O'Flaherty and Major Derry in the Vatican I found that they knew all about it already and a good deal more that I didn't know, namely that the other two flats had also been raided.

It was the porter who had betrayed us. He had done it for money and since the bounty was the equivalent of about £150 per head at the 1943 rate of exchange and there were perhaps 80–90 prisoners involved, it must have been quite a fortune to a poor porter, and was certainly a temptation to which he should never have been subjected.

There was a slight air of incredulity in some quarters when they heard about my escape and although still trusted by the Monsignor and Major Derry, I was suspected in some quarters and some people may have thought that I was the chap who gave the whole thing away.

'He was the only one to get away.'

'Speaks German too.'

Lodzi and Nora had much work to do warning their friends and allies of what had happened and also trying to find out what had happened to those arrested. The most serious blow of all from my point of view was the loss of Franko, who had been separated from the others. We later learnt that he had been tortured in the Via Tasso torture chambers and finally shot.

The raids on all three of the Vatican flats sent violent shock waves, as you can imagine, not only through the Vatican organisation, but also through the entire underground in Rome. I was not the only person to feel the effects and I was asked by the Monsignor if I knew where Tug Wilson was to be found, and I thought:

'My God, has he been picked up too?'

After all Franko had found him his flat and perhaps that porter knew about it as well. But it appeared that he was still at large.

When I first met him Tug had decided that it was high time for him to make a move to safer accommodation and he hit on the idea of casting himself upon the altar at St. Peter's and demanding sanctuary. This he did only to be seized by the seat of his pants by two strapping Swiss Guards, given the old heave-ho and deposited on the steps outside and told to buzz off. Tug was furious. He immediately sat down and wrote an indignant letter to the Pope complaining about the treatment he had received at the hands of his Guards.

When the Pope got the letter he spoke to Sir D'Arcy Osborne, the British Ambassador to the Vatican, and invited Tug to meet him and promised that he would be given sanctuary. Sir D'Arcy got hold of Mons. O'Flaherty and Major Derry, who were running the POW and much other business from inside the Vatican, and they were trying to get in touch with him. I had never known where Tug hung out and I hadn't seen him since our meeting on our first day in Rome. I was glad to hear that he was making a move to safer accommodation. Later I heard that our Tug had got himself fixed up most agreeably and comfortably and didn't want to swop his creature comforts for some cell in a monastery inside the Vatican, which might well turn out to be rather too reminiscent of his old prison camp. No doubt Sir D'Arcy was able to give the Pope a diplomatic answer to his repeated requests for news of Major Wilson for he never accepted the Pope's invitation.

And now I have to write the most difficult part of this story, but you cannot write a tale about Rome without saying something about the Pope and the Vatican State. There it was, the Vatican, powerful, rich, influential, highly organised, with world-wide financial and diplomatic links, including wireless and telephone to the outside world, a ready-made information gathering and disseminating system. Absolutely all of which we lacked.

I must say that the Vatican, in the shape of Mons. O'Flaherty and Major Derry, who were I seem to remember ensconced in the Casa Teutonica (the German College), rescued us from the Communists on our arrival in Rome and they fed us and provided for our daily needs. I was never refused help when I asked for it and I am, and always will be most grateful for all that was done for us by the Monsignor and his helpers.

But the Vatican as a whole was utterly and absolutely neutral. It had to be and I understood perfectly well why even the British Ambassador had to watch his step lest the Germans used the smallest false move to step in and destroy the whole set-up.

But I felt the neutralism was more negative towards the Allies and tended to be rather less so towards the Germans. After all the Germans were fighting the Russians and keeping the atheist hordes out of Europe. I suppose they took the view that if the Pope spoke out and condemned Hitler for what he was doing to the Jews in Germany, (and they must have known what was going on) their churches would be destroyed and the Vatican itself might well be razed to the ground. They felt themselves to be the guardians of those churches and the Vatican city and its treasures. I might add that when in Rome I was asked why the Allies had done this, that or the other thing, and when the Monastery at Monte Cassino was the subject of the questions, I am afraid that my answer was to the effect that if the Pope wore trousers instead of a skirt he would have gone to Monte Cassino, taken up residence there and saved the monastery.

In case the reader may think that this is just the opinion of an ignorant fellow who doesn't know what he is talking about, it should be understood that a lot of Italians felt exactly the same way. On one occasion when the Allied Air Forces had tried to bomb a railway yard near Rome and the bombs had fallen in a working class district nearby, killing many poor people and doing a lot of damage, it was announced that the Holy Father would be visiting the scene of the destruction. There were thousands of people there when a cavalcade of great big smart shiny black cars came slowly into view, a door was opened and the Pope started to get out, but as he did so the crowd started shouting at him:–

'Why don't you do something about it?'

'Go back to the Vatican and *do* something!'

and the people started throwing stones and bottles and he was bundled quickly back into the car and driven away a lot faster than he had come. Compare that to any visit by King George VI or Winston Churchill to the East End of London during the blitz.

The Pope *must* have known what the Nazis were doing to the Jews in Germany and so, although deeply grateful to Mons. O'Flaherty and his band of brothers, I felt the Pope should have excommunicated

Hitler and any of his crew who were Catholics and that his failure to speak out and condemn their conduct was pretty contemptible.

Cesare Coen came to see me a day or two after the raid and said that for some very large sum of money – I think it was Lire 80,000, which is of course peanuts today – he could get his fiancée out of gaol. I went and got a Bankers Order for this sum and gave it to Cesare, who came back to me the next day and asked for it to be changed into two sums of L40,000. I suppose two people had to be bribed. I did this somewhat unwillingly as I rated the chances of success to be very poor, handed over the money, and that was the last I saw of Cesare and the money and needless to say no fiancée ever turned up in Rome.

However after the war I got a letter from Cesare who wrote to me from Palestine via the War Office asking for another enormous sum of money, for what exact reason I can't remember, but I suppose he held me responsible for his fiancée's arrest and for failing to rescue her, and I sent the claim to the British Military Government in Italy who may have considered it as part of my legitimate expenses, but I doubt it.

IX

'WHEN IN ROME . . .'

On losing my residence, my friends, my supply of food and Franko, I had to stand on my own feet and for the next six months I lived and operated by relying on the people I had got to know during the Via D.Chelini days and others I came to know later.

My life during this period became extremely complicated. Some very peculiar things went on in Rome and I got mixed up in most of them. It is difficult to render them down into a consecutive story, but some description of life in Rome and the problems of living in the enemy's capital without any resources must be included. I think that, apart from Major Derry, who operated from inside the Vatican, there cannot have been many other British POWs operating in Rome, although there were plenty in hiding, and this led to all sorts of complications.

One or two of my Italian friends used to go out of Rome regularly coming back with food and other goods, riding in the back of lorries or in trains or buses and they sold their stuff on the black market, on which we all more or less relied in Rome. But black market merchandise was not the only thing they brought with them.

When in the countryside they heard about and no doubt met Allied POWs hiding in the mountains or on farms and when they learnt there was a British officer operating in Rome they sent messages, piteous messages many of them, asking for help. Some wanted money, some medical assistance, clothes, boots, news (English papers or magazines) help of every kind. I went to Monsignor O'Flaherty who was in a position to get the local priest to give help and who also gave me money and much good advice. But I had been through this business of living in caves and barns myself and, although I would have preferred to concentrate on collecting information, I could not ignore the cries for help and responded to them as best I could. If no help was sent then the poor chap would presumably just have to give himself up when he could no longer cope with his problems. And my goodness there were some problems! There was a Negro soldier who needed new boots and he took size 14 or bigger. All we could do was to get his enormous boots repaired with old car tyres. There was one fellow, a Sergeant, with about thirty ex-prisoners in the mountains not too far from Rome and, as far as I could make out, he ran his show just like it had been in the Prison Camp – Reveille – Roll Call – Lights Out and so on. When he heard of me in Rome he sent me a nominal roll of his chaps together with an indent for the items they needed and, quite oblivious of the danger, he insisted on sending me a receipt for the money and for such items as I had been able to procure. I hope that he and his men survived until the arrival of the Allies when I am sure he would have astonished them by having his men all lined up, saluted smartly and reported his unit present and correct.

I was already in touch with the VIII Army by wireless and, although the organization was makeshift and tenuous, I knew I was getting through because I received answers to my messages. For instance, when the Anzio landing took place on 22nd January 1944 I sent a signal saying that I proposed to get on a bike and ride there as it seemed the simplest thing in the world, there being no German troops sealing off the bridgehead, and the whole of my efforts since leaving camp had been directed to that end. But I got a signal back pretty smartly telling me to stay put and carry on the good work, which was very encouraging.

When I got the signal to stay in Rome I was very pleased that somebody thought that what I was doing was useful and I was quite happy to stay, since in common with everyone else in Rome, I thought that the Allies, now less than 25 miles from the centre of the city, would arrive in about a fortnight. None of us ever dreamed that we should have to await their arrival for nearly six months. Had I known that I would have to stick it out for such a long time, I think I would have got on that bike and peddled off to Anzio despite the instructions to remain in Rome.

I have not mentioned the battles fought by the American V Army and the British VIII Army firstly at Salerno, then past Naples and on northwards to the Cassino position and then Anzio, battles in which the Battalion I started the war with, the 1st Bn The Green Howards, took part. The 4th Green Howards, in which I was serving when I was captured was, of course, annihilated with the rest of 150 Brigade of 50 Div. in the Ghazala battle, but the remaining two Brigades of 50 Div. fought their way forward from Alamein and took part in the Sicily landings, but had now been withdrawn to England to prepare for Operation Overlord – the Normandy landings in which they also fought.

I have not mentioned all this here because I took no part in it, and I hope I shall be excused for not referring to the bloody battles and costly actions, which were going on daily, and which took the lives of many of my friends and comrades. I was, however, acutely aware of them, particularly in Rome, where we listened anxiously every night for news of an Allied advance, and from where I could see the AA tracer lighting up the night sky over Anzio from the balcony of Nora's flat and hear the thunder of the bombardments and bombing.

During the time we were in the Via D.Chelini flat I went out every day, the main purpose of my daily expeditions, apart from finding my way about Rome, being to meet people and try to find friends who would hide and accommodate one or all of us in case anything went wrong. By the time the flat was raided I had already found a number of absolutely trustworthy families who could be relied upon and would have been able to look after Sandy, Jack, Marcus and myself. It was to these contacts that I now turned and these marvellous people fed me, put me up and washed my clothes, accepting the appalling danger in which this placed them for the next six months until the Allies arrived in Rome in early June 1944.

There was another reason why I was intent on foraging around and meeting people. I could speak German, I had studied the German Army and could recognise the badges worn by German officers and soldiers and could therefore identify units and be in a position to send information to the Allies. As I got around I met people who supplied me with all kinds of information. I knew a chap who gave the details of all the rail traffic passing through Rome. I met Italian officers on the run and I had one living on nearly every main road in and out of Rome and they kept watch for and reported all military convoys. And, of course, there was Daniele ensconced in the German security Headquarters. I didn't want to hide and be walled up as some POWs were, I wanted to be active and do something to help, and I was able to send a lot of varied information to the Allies, and also help other less fortunate prisoners living in the mountains outside Rome.

The reader may think that it must have been very difficult for a foreigner to get around, meet and get to know so many people in such a short time. Well in Rome in 1943/44, it was absurdly easy. A British officer, any British officer, was the most sought after chap you could possibly imagine. Do you know we were saleable? I used to go to lawyers acting for prosperous clients who were doing very well out of Mussolini's government contracts, and borrow money in exchange for a chit saying that I, a British POW, had been given the money. This IOU would be produced as evidence that the client had been supporting the Allies all the time. They would pay large sums to anyone who could produce a live POW whom they could hide in their house, and I wondered if perhaps Franko had been paid for placing Tug Wilson with some Italian family and was hoping to make some more out of Sandy, Jack, Marcus and me. This was called a 'doppio gioco', in Rome, and all the big fish had some kind of proof that they were running with the hare, whilst doing very nicely with the hounds. And so it was that a British Major, who could speak Italian and move around freely in Rome, was, if not a celebrity, definitely a somebody.

There was, however, one matter which made life for me very difficult and which I felt deeply about. In the raids on the Vatican flats I was the only one to escape. It was known in the Vatican that I spoke German because I used to act as Franko's interpreter, and I suppose it was only natural and perhaps prudent that people in the POW business in Vatican circles should say a word of warning about me. I noticed a change in the attitude of some people and when a door which had formerly opened with a warm welcome was slammed in my face I felt the blow very severely. For example, one of my safe houses was a flat in which an Italian Count was being looked after by a delightful little film actress, who was out of a job as there were virtually no films being made in Rome. The Count who was described by his girlfriend as 'molto Conte' which must be a '5 star Count' was not living in our world at all. He was writing romances about knights rescuing maidens immured in castles by wicked Barons, and had to be well fed to supply the inspiration for these flights of imagination and perhaps also for other reasons.

Staying in their flat one night I heard and saw a column of tanks and other Army vehicles passing my window. I identified and counted them and next day I could see the marks made by the tank tracks in the road, so I borrowed a bicycle and followed the tracks to a wooded area some 15km south of Rome, peddled back and sent a message suggesting that the RAF might do something about that wood.

The next time I stayed in this flat the word must have got round that I was a somewhat suspect person and the little lady decided to put me to the test. The next morning for breakfast she produced a large plate of beetroot. This was an unusual meal but like all good soldiers I will eat almost anything and I was in no position to refuse a square meal when it was offered me, so I ate it, said 'Thank you very much' and sallied forth about my daily business. But my hostess, who had been introduced to me through the Vatican organisation, decided then and there that I really was a German and the next time I came to the flat the door was slammed in my face and no doubt she spread the story around which did not make life any easier for me. Her 'molto Conte' did in fact write one tale, which told of the stirring events which were going on all round him in Rome, but since this story was about me and it was written after I had been shut out of the flat, it was probably inspired by the 'beetroot breakfast' incident in which I must have appeared as a German spy and a dangerous double agent. I wondered what kind of a story his imagination would lead him to write when prompted by such powerful real life inspiration.

Needless to say when I had found my feet and established myself in Rome I realised the importance of having Daniele in the SS and looking back on it afterwards perhaps I owed my safety in Rome more than a little to him. I didn't need to do anything much about him because he and Nora already had excellent working arrangements. I therefore did very little business with Daniele and left all that to Nora. The sort of information we would get from him would be about raids to be carried out on the underground in Rome. From Daniele, Nora would often get warning of a raid, an impending arrest, a house which was being watched, or a tapped telephone line and of course she would go and warn the Communists or the people concerned.

'Look, Professor, you are suspected of this and that, your flat is going to be raided next Saturday and searched for evidence.'
The raid would be carried out on Saturday night with Daniele taking part and there they would find bags of nails for puncturing tyres, explosives or explosive literature of the most damning kind, and the Professor would be carted off to gaol. And then what do you think happened next? Professor would smuggle out a note to say:
'I was betrayed. Daniele took part in the raid. He is a traitor and must be eliminated.'

You must remember that in 1943 Stalin was regarded as the saviour of Russia. His power and influence reached their apogee with the defence of Stalingrad. He was the Little Father and was universally worshipped in Russia. He was also worshipped by the Italian Communists, who used the sign of the baffone ⌐(Stalin's moustache) as a secret sign in much the same way as the early Christians used the sign of the cross during the persecution. The Communists used to perform ceremonies round the baffone, marching or dancing round while a declamation or a speech was being made. All of this was done in great secrecy at their clandestine meetings.

There must have been at least three occasions when we warned the Communists that a raid would take place. No notice was taken of our warnings and the raid took place exactly as we had foretold and in each case we were held to be traitors, people to be shunned, despicable and so on.

I think the Communist set-up was so monolithic, yet cell-like and preoccupied with security, that it wasn't very good at passing a warning rapidly around Rome to the right quarter. Even when the warning was delivered directly to the person concerned I dare say it all had to be referred to HQ before any action could be taken. None of us liked the Communists, and it was mutual, they making it quite clear that they were not on our side. They did not help or co-operate with us in any way at all. Their mistrust and failure to act on our warnings, and their very unfriendly reception of us on our arrival in Rome all compounded my dislike. Nora, of course had memories of escaping from Russia as a girl and had lost everything in the process. But we had to work with them as they were much the largest and the only well organised underground movement in Rome.

The friends and acquaintances I had made in my daily expeditions were now my sole means of support and I had somehow to make a secure, safe mode of living from my existing circle and to expand it, change it and cut out parts of it, as the need arose to cope with the ever-changing situation in Rome. The system I built up worked like this. I would start with someone I could trust absolutely, Nora, Captain Trippi, Franko, Monsignor O'Flaherty in the Vatican or someone like that. Let us call this person A. Through him or her I would meet B, through B I would meet C and eventually D. If I trusted D completely I would make use of him or her and have nothing more to do with B and C. I thus established a cut-off which meant that if any one member in my chain was caught and tortured there would be no link connecting me to anyone else or them to each other.

There was also the danger that someone might be caught in a rastrellamento (cordon and search operation), be put in prison and be in possible danger of being shot as a hostage, even if entirely innocent. The mother would be desperate to get her boy out of prison and might have the idea of giving me away in exchange for her son. After all, I was a prisoner of war and would not be shot, her son would and was obviously infinitely more precious to her. If that mother happened to be an A or a D I had to drop her like a hot cake and cultivate another A or D to replace her.

Sometimes this system operated well and at other times with great difficulties or I only operated it with the greatest reluctance. I remember one B family very well. They were Danish – a nobleman, and I met them through Nora, an A if ever there was one. I remember Nora telling me that I was invited to a party at their flat. I said I didn't want to go, I hadn't any decent clothes, what language would I speak, who would I have to pretend to be among a bunch of strangers?

'Oh, just say you're Danish.'

'But I've never been to Denmark and I can't speak a word of Danish.'

'Just say you were educated in England; they all speak English. You'll be OK.'

I don't think that I am particularly good at cocktail parties at the best of times and I expect I was pretty uncouth at this one, but as a foraging exercise I thought perhaps I ought to go. One might meet some interesting people.

They were the most charming people, speaking English as well as I and lived in a different social circle from Nora in another part of Rome. Apart from the fact that I was asked my opinion, and had to try and talk intelligently about Danish cities, institutions, parks, theatres or whatever, not even being sure what it was I was talking about, I think I coped reasonably well. I expect I put my foot in it properly and you can imagine the sort of thing, when someone is talking about something Danish and I hadn't a clue if it was a Brewery or an Opera House. . . . ! But I am sure I was rumbled from the beginning and they were too polite to let on. They were ideal contacts. But they were in the B position so I dropped them straight away when the need arose and cultivated a very attractive animated little Italian lady whom I met at the party.

My Italian poppet was in the C position. Here it was very hard to bring down the chopper because she took to me in a big way and of course rapidly twigged who I really was. She gave me a suit of her husband's clothes, and there seemed to be quite a good prospect of stepping into the husband's shoes as well, and I am sure that this would have been most agreeable. But the prospect of being caught embracing his wife in his own suit would, I thought, not be well received. And, since I was looking for somewhere to spend the night, his suit might lead to his pyjamas and where that would lead to didn't need any guessing at all. However that might have been she was in the C position so, when, through her I met an Italian Army officer's wife, whose husband was serving somewhere in the Balkans and who hadn't heard from him for about four months, I dropped my dear little provider of the suit and took up with Signora D who turned out to be as brave as a lion and most useful in all kinds of ways until her house was watched and her telephone was tapped and I couldn't go there any more and had to start the whole process all over again.

Signora D was in fact a German lady, married to Captain Chiarizia who at that time was missing somewhere in the Balkans. She was an ardent anti-Fascist and would have gone up to General Kesselring and asked him what he was planning to do next if I had asked her to do so. She was quite without fear, to such an extent, that it made me somewhat apprehensive at the thought of what she might get up to next. Her name was Anneliese.

One day I was lying on the grass in a quiet part of the Villa Borghese park in the dappled shade of a tree, looking up at the beautiful blue sky and no doubt wondering where my next meal was coming from. I was waiting for Anneliese, who did eventually arrrive, but soon afterwards the park seemed to fill rapidly with Carabiniéri who advanced towards me across the grass. It was a rastrellamento. To run away would have been stupid so I awaited their arrival and stood up when they came up to me and asked for my papers. I showed them my identity card and gave as my address a bombed-out house in Rome and, since, I spotted immediately that the policeman who was questioning me was a Neapolitan I replied in my best South Tyrrol Austrian dialect, which I had picked up with the Austrian Army in 1937. I also showed him a certificate to show that I was a mobilised member of the War Wounded Rehabilitation organisation and my Identity Card which said I was a sculptor by profession. If they were looking for deserters of military age I expect my balding head made me look older than I really was and however it was, I got away with it. So, with my heart thumping almost audibly, I managed to saunter unconcernedly away with Anneliese who was not questioned. I wrote to Anneliese after the war hoping to see her again when I took my family to Italy to see the scenes I have tried to describe in this account, but I never received an answer to my letter and so I have lost touch with her.

When I told Nora of the dangers lurking in the Villa Borghese Park I refrained from mentioning that I had been with Anneliese because,

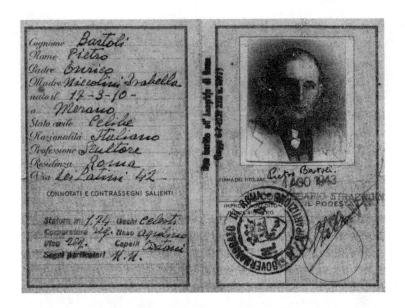

COMMISSARIATO NAZIONALE DEL LAVORO

UFFICIO PROVINCIALE DI ROMA - SERVIZIO COLLOCAMENTO

Roma, 12-4-1944

Si dichiara che il Signor *Bartoli Pietro*

Es wird hiermit bestätigt, dass Herr

abitante in *Roma*

wohnhaft in

precettato con Cartolina Nr. *278/23* è stato esentato dal servizio obbligatorio del lavoro.

vorgeladen mit Karte Nr für den Arbeitseinsatz z.Zeit nicht verwandbar ist.

1) Malato dal per la durata di

Krank seit dem für die Dauer von

2) Inidoneo al lavoro perchè

Arbeitsunfähig wegen

3) Soldato da

Soldat seit dem

4) Al lavoro presso *C.N. Prat. Edil. General.*

In Arbeit bei

IL CAPO DELL'UFFICIO COLLOCAMENTO

Mod. J - SC.

as a Russian she had no love of Germans and she also didn't approve of my association with Anneliese, so I told her that I was lying on the grass fast asleep when I was caught in the rastrellamento. She gave me a tremendous ticking off for being fast asleep and getting myself caught so stupidly. When she asked how I managed to get away she roared with laughter at the thought that I had terrified the poor little Neapolitan policeman by speaking German to him!

After meeting Nora's Danish friends and attending their party at which everyone was very well dressed, I became acutely aware of the ill-fitting oddments in which I was walking about Rome and I was told that I must go to Ciro who was not only the best tailor in Rome but who became one of my best friends. Everybody who was anybody in Rome knew Ciro Giuliano. He was *the* tailor and he had a discreet establishment in the Corso d'Italia between the Via Veneto and the Piazza Fiume, where Nora lived. He was Count Ciano's tailor and loved to tell stories of Ciano's love of England (he was of course Mussolini's Foreign Minister and his son-in-law). Ciro's establishment comprised several fitting rooms and his staff were devoted to him. He lived near the Via D.Chelini with his youthful and very beautiful wife, whom he neglected abominably. He was a small, thin, active fellow, very quick and hard-working. His main complaint was the non-availability of good English cloth. He was a workaholic, with very little other interest in life. Again I have to say that it would have been very easy for me to have consoled Signora Ciro, but in view of the fact that he was an absolute A and in addition was the source of much information as well as the provider of suits and overcoats, I had to resist the temptation and I never in fact spent a night at their flat, although I had some very nice meals there.

Ciro gave me a smart, warm overcoat and made me a very smart suit which I wore for years after the war, and for which he would not take a penny, even after the arrival of the Allies when I was in funds at last. I did however, manage to pay for a suit he made for me after the war, when we visited Rome in 1961.

Quite early on my activities attracted the attention of the authorities and I would get warnings:

'Get out of Rome – they are after you.'

Despite such warnings, as I knew few people outside Rome and had no wish to go back to living in barns, caves etc on the mountains in winter and I had my system, I stayed in Rome. But since I was gathering information and transmitting it to the Allies I knew that, if I was caught, the Germans could stick me up against a wall and shoot me and it wouldn't do much good to say 'But I am a POW'. And so I thought up the idea of creating for myself another identity. I went to the International Red Cross organisation in Rome which had the particulars of all known POWs in Italy, and there by great good fortune I met Lina Gelardi. I asked her for the particulars of a chap I had known in Campo 29 who was about my size and shape and who I thought had probably gone to Switzerland. He was Major Peter Birkin and I learnt his date and place of birth, the name of his parents, his home address, Army number etc off by heart and, when I got a false identity card I gave the name Pietro Bartoli to support my story and I started using Pietro as a pseudonym instead of Dario. (Sorry, Peter, but I couldn't very well ask your permission.)

Lina was a marvellous person. She was British and, believe it or not, had been at school with my sister in England. Her father ran the Carlton Hotel in London and her brothers were both in the British Army, one of them, a Gunner Captain, was one of the first British officers I met in Rome when he came to visit Lina after the arrival of the Allies. Lina spoke Italian fluently, but with such a strong English accent that it made me quite nervous when speaking to her over the telephone which was often tapped in Rome, My accent was pretty good and I could even manage some dialects, my Tuscan being pretty convincing. She had a couple of black cocker spaniels, which she used to exercise in the Pincio Gardens where we would meet and talk about England in English and have a picnic meal, all of which did me a power of good. Sometimes these al fresco meetings were not a complete success. Once, when I had arranged to meet her, she with the dogs and picnic basket and me with my bundle of dirty underwear which her maid used to wash and mend for me, it was pouring with rain. There we sat huddled together under her umbrella, Lina complaining that I had hogged too much of the brolley causing her to get a wet bottom, but so had I. The dogs didn't think much of it either and I thought that if anyone had seen us they would have said:

'Good heavens! They must be British! Only the British would be sitting in the rain like that.'

I have called her Lina Gelardi. This was her maiden name. She was married to a Fascist official, Signor Tufaroli. Needless to say I never met him and matters had to be carefully arranged so that this didn't accidentally occur when I stayed at her flat. Since he was a Government offcial, the flat was a super safe place for me to go to. It was an extensive flat near the Piazza del Popolo and adjoining it was a small apartment belonging to Renzo Chiovenda, who rarely came to Rome and it was to Renzo's apartment that I went when Signor Tufaroli was due home.

Her flat was handy to the Pincio Gardens where she could exercise her beloved spaniels. She loved those dogs which, in her unhappy marriage, reminded her of her home in England. Indeed I remember saying to her:

'Lina, the only thing that worries me about you is that if one of those dogs gets arrested you might denounce me to get him back.'
Lina was so British in her ways. She didn't actually walk about Rome wearing red, white and blue and carrying a Union Jack, as one Italian lady did when some British POWs were marched past her house, but she took no trouble to conceal the fact that she was British through and through, which of course was precisely the opposite of my behaviour. She was a marvellous person and without her I do not think I could have stuck it out.

It was to this haven, to Lina and the little bit of England she carried about with her, that I crept when the hunt got too hot for me at the beginning of June 1944. I was there when the Americans arrived in the Piazza del Popolo and it was in her flat a week later that I met her brother Captain Gelardi, RA, when he came to visit his sister in Rome.

I had been sending messages to Allied HQ by means of a heterogeneous collection of organisations in which I had no very great confidence and of which I was sure the Allies could not have had a very high opinion. But all this changed dramatically with the arrival of Pietro (I never discovered his surname) in Rome. He arrived some time in March, and it was Pietro who rousted me out rather than the other way round. He told me that he had been sent to Rome to establish a 'Centrale' (literally a telephone exchange but in fact it was an organisation using a number of wireless sets which moved around in Rome and transmitted messages to the Allies).

Until I met him I had been forced to rely on people who claimed to have wireless or other links with the Allies, but I never knew for sure if my messages were getting through or even if they were going in the right direction. I didn't have a great deal of confidence in my contacts, who appeared to me to be rather amateurish and I felt it would be pretty stupid to stick one's neck out for nothing if the information was not getting through. I also thought that the Allies would not value the information they got from me when it arrived from such organizations.

I knew that some of my information had got through and I think that

Pietro had been told to check me out when he arrived in Rome, and if I was OK to make contact. He had apparently passed through the German front line and looked to be the sort of chap who could do it. He was a short, square stocky man, a regular Italian Army Artillery Captain of North Italian stock. He had an air of quiet competence about him and was completely free of the bombastic boastfulness of some of the people I had met who claimed to have been dropped behind the lines and were going to win the war single-handed with a six-shooter and a stick or two of gelignite. He was not at all the voluble, excitable Latin-type, but was a calm and confident influence in the rather tense and turgid atmosphere in which we operated in Rome. I thought the VIII Army could not have chosen a better chap.

But of course I could not be sure about him and I had a certain reputation to live down in some quarters in Rome and so I said to him:

'You say you are in touch with the Allies and I say I am No. 44131, Major d'A. Mander. Let us be sure of one another. I will ask you two questions the answers to which can only come from England and the British must ask me a question, which only I can answer. My questions are:

'What is my wife's maiden name, and what is our dog's name?' My wife's maiden name they might possibly get from my papers but I reckoned they would have to go to my wife and ask her:

'Is that Major Mander's dog?'

'It is, is it? What do you call it?' and that they might then say:

'Oh by the way we've had news of your husband and he is alive and kicking in Rome.'

Not a bit of it, they found out the answers and never said a word to my wife or family. Back came the answers spot on and pretty quick and with them came a very good question from the War Office.

'Where did you learn to ski?'

I had attended a Winter Warfare Course with the Czech Army in the Carpathians and my record said that I was 'qualified to lead armies over mountains in winter' and so my answer went back:

'Strbske Pleso, Czechoslovakia.' Which must have given the cypher breakers and maybe the wireless operators a bit of a headache.

Having each established our bona fides we made arrangements to communicate with one another and my contact with him was his girl friend Rosina, whom I arranged to meet periodically and whom I could generally get hold of in an emergency. Later when I had a lot of stuff to send I used to meet her every day and sometimes even more often when news was coming in hot and fast.

We varied our meeting places, sometimes at a restaurant, sometimes in the Pincio Gardens, but my favourite place was the Zoo where someone wandering around looking at the animals did not and could not arouse suspicion. We would meet at the wolves or the parrot house, embrace, hold hands and whisper as lovers do and she would take my messages and I would receive my instructions and warnings. We also swapped information about the goings on in Rome, who had been arrested, what had happened to so and so, what the Yugoslavs were up to and of course arranged our next meeting.

One day Pietro came himself to our rendezvous, which he had never done before, and I feared that he was the bearer of bad news. Actually he had an instruction, which seemed to be addressed generally to Allied agents in Rome, which was to the effect that information was required about the organisation the Germans were planning to leave behind in Rome, when they were finally driven out.

I nodded my head vigorously and started to hold forth upon the subject when Pietro said:

'Go on reading – finish the message.' It went on:

'Volunteer can interest himself in this matter.'

I was Volunteer.

At first I was rather disappointed at receiving this instruction. I was rather proud of my little band of information gatherers and I had hoped that my identification of units and German Generals, who used to frequent Ciro's establishment, traffic movements and so on was of use. To be told to concentrate on counter-intelligence work rather damped my enthusiasm. Then it dawned on me that they must have got wind of my connection with Daniele and the SS and I suddenly realized that they must be very well informed about what was going on in Rome, and knew more about me and what I was up to than I realised. The more I thought about it the more encouraged I felt. Looking back on it now I think the Allies must have had a large number of people sending them the kind of stuff I was unloading every day and that my messages were probably mainly confirmatory, but I dare say there were not many German speakers who had a pal in the SS. Somehow I thought they didn't just send that message because I spoke German. I wrote my reply:

'With great pleasure. The matter is already in hand.'

And I set to work on Daniele with Nora.

That message had ended with a chilling warning:

'Volunteer must take more care.'

This was the reason Pietro had brought it himself and he read me quite a lecture on the danger into which I would bring everybody else if I got caught. Operating wireless sets, which could be located by direction-finding instruments, was a very dangerous occupation, but it was Pietro who got caught and was shot, and I was only able to continue to send messages through the remaining operators of the Centrale which he had set up.

The most important message which Pietro transmitted for me concerned an attack on the Anzio beachhead and the information was obtained and transmitted in the following manner.

Lodzi and I used to meet for a drink in various bars, coffee houses and hotels in Rome and one of our favourite haunts was the bar in the Hotel Eden, which was very popular with the German Army and particularly that part of it which was nearest to Rome and on the Anzio front. One Saturday morning Lodzi and Nora noticed a large crowd causing quite a commotion outside the Hotel Eden and they decided to go and see what it was all about. As they approached the lobby they were told that nobody was allowed in, but since they knew a Polish lady who lived in the Hotel and were frequent visitors, well known to the hotel porter, he admitted them. While Nora went up to see her friend, Lodzi went into the lounge, which was full of German Officers and there he listened to what was the plan of attack, which was to be mounted on the Anzio beach head on Monday morning. He did not stay to hear more, but collected Nora and set out to find me in order to get the message transmitted in time.

By the time he found me it was Saturday afternoon and I had somehow to get hold of Pietro. I had never had such a hot piece of information before but I had no assignment with Rosina until Monday by which time it would all be over. Also I had no means of getting hold of Pietro that weekend. Nora suggested an Italian lady,* who I knew was sheltering a British Officer, and to my astonishment it seemed she

---

* In addition to sending information to the Allies via Pietro, this remarkable lady was sheltering a British Brigadier General more or less openly in her house. She used to go out for walks with him and, as a disguise, he had his left arm encased in plaster so as to look like a wounded soldier. I was told that after months in plaster his poor arm was sadly wasted away, but however that may have been there were some most interesting signatures and messages on that plaster when the time came to take it off with the arrival of the Allies in Rome.

<u>C O P Y</u>

<u>THE DISTINGUISHED SERVICE ORDER</u>

<u>Major (temporary) D'Arcy John Desmond MANDER (44131)</u>

<u>The Green Howards</u>
<u>(Alexandra, Princess of Wales's Own Yorkshire Regiment)</u>

This officer was taken prisoner in Africa and
transferred to Italy, but succeeded in escaping from
the train, in which he was being moved to another camp,
and eventually arrived in Rome in December 1943.

Here he got into touch with a pro-Allied Italian
intelligence organisation, which was transmitting
military intelligence by wireless to the Allies in
Southern Italy.

Major Mander himself obtained a considerable
amount of valuable information, including the date on
which the main German counter-attack would be launched
against the Anzio Bridge-head.

He also did useful work for a period of six
months in the counter-intelligence field, in the course
of which he showed great ability, resource and courage,
the result of which was the virtual elimination of
enemy agents within a short time after the capture
of Rome.

Major Mander was twice arrested by the Gestapo
and only succeeded in freeing himself by the greatest
ingenuity.

- - - - - - - - -

was doing a great deal more than that, because through her we got hold of Pietro. But Pietro had to open up the Centrale – it was Saturday evening – he would do his best, he could not be sure . . .

I was prey to horrible doubts. Were my messages getting through, would this one get through? If it did get through, would it be believed?

Not only were there people in Rome who suspected that I was a German stool pigeon, but Nora and I were also compromised in the eyes of the Communists because they knew of our association with Daniele.

If Pietro did manage to get the message away at the weekend and if it did arrive, would it be acted on? If it got to the beachhead, where no doubt alarms of every kind were of almost daily occurrence, would they take it seriously, could they get it to the front line in time and would the men stand to and the guns be ready or would it be dismissed as just another scare?

I had a most worrying weekend, but on Monday Rosina told me that Pietro had got the message away and there was no rejoicing in the local papers or talk of any kind of victory or success so I imagined that Anzio had survived. My credit at GHQ was evidently better than it was in Rome. The message got through alright and was no doubt confirmed from other sources. It was acted upon and the attack was beaten off. This one achievement made the whole of my efforts in Rome during the seven months I was there tremendously worthwhile, but it was not until after the Allies arrived in Rome that I was to find out if my small voice had been heard.

Nora told me after the war that when talking to an American officer about this message he told her that when it was received one fellow said 'Boloney', but someone else said 'I think we ought to be ready' and they were.

This business of taking more care, which was the subject of Pietro's lecture to me at our last meeting, was a very serious matter. People who were caught, and three of my close associates were caught during the time I was in Rome, were beaten and tortured in a building in the Via Tasso and, if they hadn't died under the treatment they had been subjected to, they were shot. None of the three gave anything away under the appalling treatment they received.

I had thought that if I got caught I could always claim that I was a prisoner of war, but I knew that if you wanted the Germans to put you back in prison camp one should be in uniform and not sending messages in code wearing civilian clothes. Under these circumstances I was more likely to be shot as a spy. It probably appeared to both Allied HQ and Pietro that I went about all over Rome in rather too casual a manner, but I felt that to behave perfectly normally was very good cover. My motto was 'When in Rome . . . .'

I used to frequent the area around the German HQ at the Hotel Eden. One reason was that I thought it would be the last place they would think of looking for a run-away POW and for another the electricity and water supply worked better in that area, the lifts would probably be functioning and of course, one saw more Germans and could make more identifications from their uniforms.

I have already described the system whereby all my safe-house families were kept separate. None of the A's or D's knew each other and the B's and C's had been dropped so as to create a good layer of insulation. I also kept those who supplied me with information separate from those who provided me with my safe-house accommod-ation. My contacts were scattered all over Rome and came from every strata of society from counts and countesses to butchers, bakers and candlestick makers, so that there would be no thread that anyone could follow which would lead them to me. This system served me well and I was able to survive from the time of our arrival in Rome at the end of November 1943 until the arrival of the Allies in early June 1944.

It was not, however, a solid cast-iron arrangement and had to be changed, sometimes pretty rapidly, to meet emergencies. For example an event staged by the Communists in March 1944 produced effects which required me to take immediate action about my security arrangements. The Communists had been urging other anti-fascist underground groups to fight and liberate Rome, probably because they thought the Allies would arrive in a few days and save them the bother. But the Allies didn't come and it became obvious that they were not going to arrive for some considerable time, so, in order to justify all their propaganda, they felt they had to do something and not just behave, as they accused everyone else of behaving, in supine inactivity. So on 23rd March 1943 they planted a bomb in the Via Babuino, a street used regularly by German troops and, as 156 German soldiers were returning to their barracks, they set it off, killing 33 of them. Immediately the Italian Police were ordered to retaliate by picking up 330 Italians, who were then transported to the Ardeatine Caves in lorry loads of fifty and shot, five at a time in the back of the head. This caused considerable panic in Rome for a time, but when it was realised that the Germans had taken their ten pounds of flesh, calm returned once more, and a great deal less was heard from the Communists and other firebrands about taking up arms against the Germans.

This incident had a very direct effect on my security system. One of the hostages was the son of one of my safe-house families and they were desperate to get him back. I therefore had to drop them like a hot potato in case they had the idea of swopping me for the boy. After all they could say I was a POW who would only be put back in prison camp and would not be shot.

The Via Babuino bomb also caused me much anxiety because it was in this road, near where the bomb went off, that one of my most valued helpers lived. He was Dr Lenart, a Jewish surgeon from Vienna, who had fled with his Austrian wife to Italy at the time of the Anschluss. He was a brilliant surgeon and he lived an underground existence in Rome by performing operations which were beyond the competence of Italian surgeons. He was paid a fee for doing the work and the Italian surgeon got the credit for the result. Dr Lenart was a mine of information and a most enthusiastic anti-Nazi. Through him I got in touch with the Jewish underground who helped me in various ways and I was able to get them a wireless transmitter from the Italian Air Force which was capable of being heard in Tunis. Dr Lenart lived in a studio flat in the Via Babuino where I had spent the night and many happy hours talking about Vienna and the Austria that I knew so well before the Anschluss. I feared that the Lenarts might be caught in a rastrellamento of the Via Babuino area after the bomb, but miraculously they had survived and he carried on, not only with his undercover medical work but also with his anti-Nazi, pro-Allied activities.

I have already mentioned the problems posed by prisoners in the mountains outside Rome, one of these poor chaps was ill from what sounded like diabetes. I was able to get Dr Lenart to go out to see him, he confirmed that it was diabetes and arranged for the man to have insulin injections and treatment and visited him periodically. I also remember one day he was very excited because he had seen a Vienna bus, obviously requisitioned by the Germans, he wanted to blow it up or set it on fire but I persuaded him to steal it and drive it into the River Tiber, which has quite high banks in Rome, and to wreck it, which he did.

Sometimes I was followed, but usually managed to shake my man off by changing trams and getting on another one going in the opposite direction before he could get off and catch the other one. Another way of shaking off a tail was to turn abruptly round and walk directly back along the pavement. This always disconcerted them. They didn't want to give themselves away by turning round too and they would generally become very interested in a shop window while I interested myself in another and finally slipped away. Another precaution I sometimes took was to go about Rome with a child. A man of military age alone might well be picked up by the police on suspicion of being a deserter or perhaps they might be looking for people to send to labour camps. Somehow being with a child allayed suspicion and was of course absolutely necessary if your Italian was not up to scratch. Tug Wilson went around with a small boy who bought him tram tickets, asked the way and vouched for him generally. In the same way I was sometimes accompanied by a little girl called Lalla Rossi. Her father was a Professor and he had a wonderful rapport with the thieves in the Trastevere area of Rome and also with the inmates of the prisons. Lalla was a solemn little girl and I discovered that she always carried a piece of chalk in her pocket.

'Lalla, why do you carry that chalk?' I asked her one day.

'To write on the walls.'

'What do you write on the walls, Lalla?'

'Morte à i Tedeschi! (Death to the Germans),' she replied.

When staying at the Rossi's house my method of escape, should it be raided, was to go up to the flat roof and do a long jump on to the roof of the house next door. I dare say that fear would have lent me wings, but I am glad to say I never had to do it. When I visited the Rossi's after the war I wanted to buy Lalla a box of chocolates and found I hadn't enough money. I never seemed to be short of money as a prisoner at large, but of course, sponging on my hosts I didn't spend much either.

Whilst on the subject of money perhaps I should explain how I went about getting this most necessary commodity. Money was, after a place to sleep, food and security, an absolute necessity. Monsignor O'Flaherty would always help, but I asked him only for money to help other prisoners outside Rome and tried to manage my own affairs without involving him in any way in my various undercover activities. On our way down to Rome we left chits asking the Allies to reward people who had helped us. In Rome I discovered that chits were a most useful source of money. I have already described how I could go to a lawyer, explain I was a British Major and he would get one of his clients to lend me money against a chit stating that he had helped me. There was also HM Ambassador to the Holy See who had a butler who would cash cheques. He cashed one of mine, and when my wife got the cancelled cheque she enquired of Messrs. Holts, our Bankers, who Mr Harris was, and was told that he was 'in the Vatican,' and my family, who hadn't had any news of me for over six months, assumed that I was safely tucked away in the Pope's pocket.

So far as food was concerned I relied greatly on my hosts. I did go and get the occasional Red Cross parcel and I also had two false ration cards, one of which was much admired by my friends – it was a very good one and, being for a pregnant woman, entitled me to many little extras not generally available in tightly rationed Rome. I was of course in touch with many black marketeers and occasionally went out of Rome and picked up some cheese, a chicken, or a joint of lamb which would be welcome to people who had been feeding me from their meagre resources. But mainly I left this business of going out of Rome to my friends who were more expert in this field of activity.

There were in Rome quite a number of foreigners – such as Franko, a Yugoslav, Nora, a Russian and Lodzi, a Hungarian. Through them I met other foreigners living perfectly legitimate existences in Rome, as well as refugees, deserters and people on the run to whom one naturally gravitated. Of all these nationalities the Yugoslavs provided me with the greatest problems. Franko introduced me to them early on and if only it had been possible to get them to direct their energies against the enemy they would have been marvellous people to work with, but they seemed only intent upon fighting each other. You had to be very careful in your dealings with them unless you knew for certain to which faction they belonged. There were Communists and Royalists, Catholics and Muslims, Serbs, Croats and Slovenes all intent on cutting each others throats. The sort of thing that would happen on meeting one of them would be that I would be asked:

'Have you seen Broz lately?'

'No. Why do you ask?'

'We have to kill him.'

In my cell in the prison camp I had a wonderful picture of General Mihailovich. I stuck it on the wall which I hoped would annoy the Italians, but I remembered his face well, and when in Rome, I tried to help the Mihailovich Party. But this led inevitably to a quarrel with the Tito side. Later on when I got back to England it was suggested that I should be dropped in Yugoslavia and put the experience I had gained in Italy to further use. However, by then my hero had been assassinated by Tito's men and I reckoned they would probably cut my throat too. Also I had had more than enough of underground activities and only wanted to be a proper soldier once again. I sometimes carried a gun but after a while I decided that it was less risky to be an unarmed civilian, besides which the chances of shooting your way out of trouble would be small.

I went under several different names in Rome. To the VIII Army I was Volunteer. To Nora's little underground group I was Orso (the Bear) and to my various friends I might be Pietro Bartoli or Dario or some other name. On one occasion I got into some difficulty in a very crowded tram – and the trams and trolley-buses in Rome were apt to be packed tighter than sardines and would sail along with a small swarm of Italians hanging on the footplate at the back. A chap in the front of the tram hailed me:

'Hallo Dario! How goes it?'

But I was with another chap in the middle of the tram who knew me as Pietro. And there were occasions when I forgot what name I had used. It could then be very awkward, if you happened to bump into someone in the street and not know your own name when you met an old friend!

I kept my various activities strictly apart. My information gatherers were mainly Italian officers on the run. I never slept in their houses, nor in the houses of those who travelled in and out of Rome bringing food and information. The black marketeers, Communists, Jews, Yugoslavs, the lawyers I got money from, all had to be kept at arm's length from each other and in the case of the Yugoslavs, persuaded that it was the Germans who were their enemies.

Apart from sleeping in a different house each night in a different part of Rome and with people in various strata of society I took other precautions. For instance, when keeping an appointment with someone I didn't know or was not sure of, or indeed any appointment, I always arrived well before the appointed hour and stationed myself so that I could command a view of the approaches to the meeting place and plan a convenient retreat. Even if it was someone I knew well and we were to meet at a restaurant in a square, I would still get there over an hour beforehand and sit at another restaurant or browse in a shop and then, as did in fact happen, if about four burly chaps appeared and took up positions around the square ostentatiously reading news-papers, I could pay my bill and walk quietly away.

In the spring of 1944 when we heard about the V1 and V2 rocket sites being built on the other side of the channel from which sites these missiles were to be fired at London, I got to hear that the Todt organization was recruiting men in Italy and indeed all over Europe, to work on the sites. Maybe things were getting to be a bit hot for me in Rome and so I sent a message volunteering to join the Todt organisation, go to work on the sites and send information back from France or Belgium, which I thought would be pretty easy to organise. Looking back on it from this distance in time it doesn't seem such a good idea because travelling, working and living with Italians on the sites every day it would have been very difficult for me to continue to pass for a native Italian, nor could I pass myself off as a Frenchman or German. I would have certainly been spotted as an odd bod and probably denounced. Also I expect our Intelligence people already had a good set-up in France which was sending them all the information they wanted about the work, and again I was told to stay in Rome and carry on the good work. But I had been there a long time and I was not as enthusiastic about staying as I had been in January, when I wanted to go to Anzio and when I expected the Allies to get to Rome in about a fortnight.

One day I was summoned urgently to the Piazza Fiume flat and had to listen to the most extraordinary tale. The Kiss's told me that Daniele's section of the SS had been deputed to plaster Rome with posters, purporting to come from the Communist Party and inciting the population to rebellion and acts of violence. Only Daniele's section knew about this. I found it hard to believe such a thing, but they had one of the posters there and they told me that they had spoken to some of their collaborators who all agreed that the Germans had chosen an excellent moment to make such a move and that it might succeed all too well.

I protested that the whole thing was too far-fetched and absurd, but I was well aware of the unnatural calm that ruled in Rome after the Ardeatine caves massacre and that the Communists and their collaborators, not friends because I don't think they had any, were lying very low. Also that there were tense, nervous elements just ready to explode, if such a spark as this were to fall on Rome. I asked why the Germans should stoop to such a thing. The answer was that the Germans felt they had lost their grip on the Communists, who they feared were building up their strength, waiting for an opportunity when it would be difficult for them to deal with unrest on their long line of communications. Whereas at that moment they were equipped and in a position to deal with the Communists if they could get their leaders out of hiding. Under such circumstances they could deal with them on their own terms.

The Kiss's wanted me to send a message to the Allies asking for the plot to be exposed on the radio along with the 'special messages'. I pointed out that, if only Daniele's Section knew of the plan, suspicion would inevitably fall on him, but I was told it was quite a big section and they felt the matter was so serious that the risk had to be taken. In the end I was persuaded to do as they asked and I arranged for a message to be sent warning the Underground to ignore the posters when they went up.

Soon after I had left the flat, the lady who lived across the way called out in an unnecessarily loud voice and asked Nora if she could lend her some sugar. Nora realised at once that something was up, so chattering loudly went to find the sugar and her friend asked her also for a sieve and whispered to her;

'They are in my flat and are coming to you next.'
and two Security Police emerged onto the landing and walked into her flat. Nora's heart was pounding. The poster lay on the sofa; there was no time to hide or destroy it, so Nora, with the sieve in her hand pushed it to one side so they could sit down and put the sieve on it. One man searched the flat and the other sat on the sofa, pushed the poster further aside with his hand, interrogated them and examined their papers. Nora kept all incriminating papers in the toes of her point ballet shoes, they also had a couple of automatic pistols which were in a pair of Lodzi's riding boots, and of course this poster was in full view with the sieve on it. The man searching the flat admired Lodzi's boots:–

'You don't get boots like that in Italy nowadays.'
He didn't find the pistols but in looking through her list of telephone numbers he came across the name of a well known black marketeer:–

'Ah ha. You know him? What might you have to do with him?'

'Look what's written underneath,' said Nora, 'Saponeti' (soap). 'He supplies us with soap.'

Eventually the two men left and Nora burnt the poster, crumbled the ashes and flushed them down the loo, although Daniele had stipulated that all copies must unfailingly be returned to him.

However, the BBC did send the warning message and the posters were never put up. The scheme was a damp squib and the whole thing collapsed, so I don't suppose the missing poster was ever required.

Thus it was that the searchers did not see what was lying under their noses. I thought that only happened in books written by Conan Doyle or Agatha Christie, but it seems to happen in real life also.

X

'MERIELA STA BENE'

'Meriel is well'

How big is a piece of soap? It is at its biggest when taken out of its wrapper and becomes smaller and thinner with use. When I arrived in Rome I had already been out of the wrapper for a considerable time but I was still a good solid useful bar of soap. Now after six months of hard use I was worn down to a miserable sliver of a thing and was hardly fit for anything.

At the end of May the interminable battle at Cassino seemed to intensify. Would they never break through? The weather got very hot and sultry and there were signs that the hunt for me was also getting uncomfortably hot. We had had some losses, particularly among the wireless operators and I seemed to be getting too well known for my own and my friends' safety. I had been given plenty of warnings to get out of Rome and it had become too dangerous to go to the Vatican. On my last visit there I was warned that Anneliese Chiarizia's flat was being watched and her telephone tapped. This news was bad enough in itself because Anneliese was a brave and a most valued friend and supporter, but what was even worse was that the Vatican boys knew of my association with her, which should have been a secret known only to us two. I felt I couldn't just ring her up and say:

'Oh, hallo, Anneliese your phone is tapped and there is someone listening to our conversation and by the way your flat is being watched,' and, since I had no appointment to see her for some time, the only thing to do was to go to her flat and warn her.

As I left the Vatican an unobtrusive figure emerged from the famous colonnade in the Piazza San Pietro and followed me out of the square, and I had to shake him off before I could go to Anneliese, all of which took some time. The entry to Anneliese's flat was in an internal quadrangle with an entrance from the street. Having arrived unescorted I walked through the street entrance and immediately saw the man who was watching the place. There was only one thing to do and that was to march briskly up to the entrance to her block, run smartly up the stairs to the third floor and deliver my message.

When I got inside I looked out of the window and spotted another fellow in the street, busy doing nothing at all, and Anneliese told me there was a third man at the back entrance. I gave Anneliese my warning, told her I would not be coming to see her again and not to try and contact me no matter how important the matter might seem. I bid her and her sister-in-law a fond, if brief, farewell, and departed as briskly as I had arrived. I passed the chap in the quadrangle, who must have given his pal outside a signal, because when I went into the street and walked to the tram stop the watcher in the street detached himself from the wall against which he was leaning and followed me. Twice in one day! I had to shake him off and then make a long trip to the other side of Rome where I was going to spend the night, all of which gave me something to think about.

You may wonder who it was that was putting a tail on me and who were the people who raided the Via D.Chelini flat and of course I had no idea. Generally speaking the Italian Police and Army, and of course all the Fascist para-military organizations, were responsible for rounding up escaped prisoners and deserters from their own armed forces, just as the Police in England try to apprehend absconders from gaol. There were also a large number of Germans who held Italy in an iron grip. They were doing nearly all the fighting at the front and they made sure that the Italians functioned in the rear areas. In Florence I was arrested by Italian Fascists and we had been denounced by an Italian. In the Via D.Chelini there were two German soldiers waiting for me. I don't know who it was who actually carried out the raid although we knew we had been given away by an Italian, the porter who was to have collected our baggage, but instead collected the L1800 that he would be paid for each prisoner he betrayed.

It was obvious that the Italian authorities were riddled with Communists and pro-Allied people, for it must be well known that the heart of the Italian people was not in the war and in general they liked the British, admired the Americans and hated and feared the Germans. Of course there were also some Germans who knew that the war was already hopelessly lost and who wanted no further part in the struggle. So the people who chivvied us around in Italy were mainly the Italian Fascisti, police and military, working under the orders of the German military and Nazi para-military organizations. They were not pleasant people and one did one's best to avoid falling into their lethal clutches.

With regard to their Intelligence organizations the Abwehr and S.I.M. (Servio Intelligenza Militare – the Italian MI6), the strange ambivalent character of Admiral Canaris is well-known and the S.I.M. was so riddled with pro-Allied people that it wouldn't surprise me to be told that a large number of my earlier messages had been sent to the Allies by the S.I.M. through their organization or with their help.

It was shortly before this that Lodzi had been arrested trying to sell gold on the black market and Nora was not merely worried she was frantic, until we heard that he was held by the Italian Police and not the Germans and we managed to get him back, shaken but otherwise nearly the same old Lodzi. We were all pretty shaken by his arrest. Lodzi wasn't tough like Nora and, if he had been taken to the Via Tasso, we feared not only for his life but also for our own, because we felt that he would not be able to withstand beating and torture and might have been forced to spill the beans.

There had also been a number of other arrests among the underground fraternity and most of the wireless operators were out of action or had simply disappeared. By this time I was again carrying an automatic. I knew they were not following me about Rome looking so assiduously for me just because I was a POW but because of my connection with Pietro's Centrale and my association with just about every dissident underground organisation in Rome. I thought that if I got caught my chances of being shipped off to another prison camp were small and that I stood a good chance of being taken to the Via Tasso. I carried that pistol and would not have hesitated to use it to avoid arrest.

The next day I set out uneasy in my mind and wondering what on earth I ought to do, when a friend of mine saw me and, obviously startled, said:

'I thought you had left Rome. You shouldn't be here, you must get away at once.'

I had had these warnings before and you may say 'Why didn't you get out? It was good advice, why not take it?' The answer is that I had no contacts outside Rome and had made no arrangements for such an eventuality. I had relied on my friends and had confidence in my system and both had stood me in good stead for six months. But now I was worried, things were beginning to catch up on me and I didn't want to get caught at the last minute and get myself and possibly my friends into trouble just when it looked as though I might be on the last lap.

Walking back through leafy residential avenues I ran into our Camp Interpreter. The Capitano must have called my name at countless Roll Calls, but he didn't seem to recognise me and I passed quietly by.

By now I had spent nine months living on the run, the last six months of which were spent in Rome like a hunted creature. The sensation is exhilarating and keeps you on your toes, but it is not a situation to be lived with indefinitely and by now it had been going on too long for me and for the first time I had the feeling that the game was up.

I arrived in the Corso d'Italia, close to Ciro's establishment. I was pretty sure I was not being followed so, when I felt a tap on the shoulder and turned around to come face to face with a German officer in uniform, I nearly shot him then and there. However he politely asked me the way to the Via Veneto, I pointed it out to him and completely forgot to send him off in the wrong direction, which was my usual habit. I went to a cafe and ordered a strong drink. What was I to do? My communications organisaton was shot to pieces and I hardly dared to go and meet the people who gathered information for me, so there was little or nothing to send even if I could have sent it.

I was close to Ciro's place but I knew that one of his closest associates had been arrested and taken to the Via Tasso. This brave Lt. Colonel in the Italian Army died under the most appalling beatings and torture without revealing a thing to his torturers, but I did not know this at the time. It was not far to Nora's flat in the Piazza Fiume, but she, the most resourceful of my friends, had been badly shaken by Lodzi's arrest, and her flat was neither the most secure nor the most comfortable place to stay. I felt I had to go to ground immediately so I decided to go to Lina and hide in Renzo's flat. There I found peace and quiet and was able to regain my nerve and recharge my batteries. I was there for one or two days lying completely doggo, so I missed seeing the ragged columns of Germans retreating through Rome, lorries with flat tyres being driven as far as they would go until they were abandoned and the crew took to their feet. And then at last Rome was still. There was no battle, no shot or shell-fire. It was eerie and as the heat of the day gave way to the cool of the evening and then at last to a brilliant moonlit night it was obvious that something was in the air. The curfew was still on and we had all long since got into the habit of spending the evenings and nights 'at home'. You didn't go out at night unless you were taken out with a gun in your ribs.

Slowly a strange small noise reached our ears, a distant crepitation, like rain falling on dried leaves. In fact it was the sound of people clapping their hands in the distance but we didn't know it. I crept out of the flat, the first time I had done such a thing since arriving in Rome. I walked quietly in the sepia shadow of the flats and houses towards the Piazza del Popolo, brilliantly lit by the light of the full moon. I went into a dark portico hidden in the deep summer night shadow. The little noise I had heard in the flat went on, the sound of distant voices could be heard. Surely there was something happening on the far side of the square. Suddenly the quiet was shattered by the firing of a gun nearby. Those people weren't Germans, who then could they be?

I stepped out from the shadow and stood for a moment in the full moonlight and then walked across the middle of the deserted square to the far side, where I saw the shape of a tank and some figures in the shadow. I said in English.

'I am a British officer, can I help you?'

'Say, Hank, here's a guy says he's a British officer and can he help.' Hank it transpired was the Commander of a Ranger Battalion of the American V Army and he replied briefly.

'Yeah, where the heck are we?'

'You are in the Piazza del Popolo: there on your map and the River Tevere is just over there. I am pretty sure the bridges are not blown or I would have heard them go up and I don't think they are defended either, but I can find out for you if you will give me a minute.'

'That's great, that's just where we're supposed to be. You go and find out about those bridges.'

I went and rang up some people who lived just over the Ponte Margherita and they confirmed that the bridge was intact and the Germans had long since departed. The Rangers moved on and their leading elements were five miles beyond Monte Mario to the north of Rome by dawn.

That night I spent helping the Americans. We established a first aid post and when they were over the river and settled I went back to Lina, and Rome awoke to the good news.

Rome had been liberated by General Mark Clark and the American V Army but I had not long been in Lina's flat before I heard that the British were in the Pincio Gardens and after a hurried wash and shave and a bite to eat I returned to the Piazza del Popolo and there, just above the spot where I had met Colonel Hank the night before I saw a small tent and in it I saw the curly ginger head of Major Cuthbert Cave who was a chap I had worked with at the War Office before the war.

'Hullo, Cuthbert.'

'Hullo, d'Arcy, glad to see you.'

But by God I was very much more glad to see him.

I had left home in the spring of 1941 and had not seen my family for over three years, and in particular, I had never seen our daughter who was born when I was in the Western Desert in 1941. Needless to say I hoped to get home as soon as possible. Most of my work in Rome was done but there remained the organization the Germans had left behind in Rome. And of course, as a pretty well-informed local inhabitant, who knew his way around Rome, I was able to be of use in small day to day matters. So I couldn't just demand a ticket back to London right away. Our people asked me to stay on in Rome to deal with the German agents and asked me what I wanted and I replied.

'Uniform.'

I also asked for money and a car to get about Rome. I wanted above all to rejoin the Army, become a proper soldier again and get back into uniform. I moved into a room at the Hotel Eden, where I encountered the American breakfast, the K ration and the American officer for the first time, and I was given a little Fiat Topolino car. I had to go down to Anzio to get uniform and some money from the Field Cashier and I also managed to get hold of some white bread, which I brought back to Rome and distributed among my friends. At Anzio I was told I had to go down to Naples to check in with the Army and the POW people, and for a medical check up, but before going there Nora and I had a go at Daniele, who appeared to be somewhat dilatory in the matter of coughing up the information we wanted about the organization the Germans had left in Rome. I am afraid that Daniele was playing the double game for all he was worth, and up to the very last. I had to get him out of gaol twice because the Communists had him arrested as an SS man, and one can quite understand that he wanted perhaps not just money but at least security in exchange for his information. But meanwhile, unknown to him, many of the Italians, who had been given money, codes, wireless sets etc with which to send information from Rome were coming in and saying they didn't want any part of the assignment and were handing over their equipment, instructions and money to us.

When, therefore, I had bailed Daniele out for the second time I told him that if he didn't hurry up and spill the beans there would be no beans left to spill. And he spilled them. So it was that the entire network the Germans had left behind fell into our hands. Our problem now was not to let the Germans know what had happened so we therefore had to use their sets to send the information that we wanted them to receive, and it was in the matter of getting these sets properly 'sistemato-ed' that I was able to lend a hand.

One or two of the wireless sets were put in one of my very best safe houses, which was about the most perfect hidey-hole you could possibly imagine. It was a bachelor pad, a penthouse flat, and the lift only went up to the floor below, unless you had a special key when it would go up to the floor above. There was also a staircase with a locked door at the bottom and the top, and also another way out by way of the fire escape, which was common to the next door building.

The owner of this flat was a delightful young fellow who came from Venice and only visited Rome periodically and I had asked him to set up an organisation in the Venice area to collect information and install one or two wireless sets up there. He agreed and we arranged Code words (yet another Messagio Speciale) and frequencies so that he could receive instructions and send messages to us. I had visions of his messages being received in his own flat in Rome but we couldn't do it that way as it was needed for talking to the Germans.

In the end we picked up every single agent they left behind, except for the head of the ring, whose name was I think Hoffman. But we never found any trace of Herr Hoffman's existence, and I came to the conclusion that he was a mythical figure invented by the Germans to keep their agents on their toes who never in fact existed at all, or, if he had existed, he must have seen how the land lay and slipped away at the last minute.

I would have liked to be able to report that Daniele and I went round with the Military Police and arrested these agents, but in fact most of them saved us the trouble. Thus it was that my work in Rome came to a rapid end, and this sudden collapse of all that I had been working for had a curious effect on me. I think it was sheer reaction. I had been hunted for so long that when the strain was released, something snapped. I couldn't sleep at night, I felt ill, my work was done, all I wanted to do was to get home.

I had to go down to Naples and I took Lodzi and Nora with me as I thought they needed a break as much as I did. We could find no accommodation in Naples, which was absolutely full up (the only rooms we could get were offered to us on an hourly basis). So we went on to Amalfi, where I had the most peculiar feeling that I had been there before. It was only when I got home and saw a picture of Amalfi in my mother's house that I realised where the delusion sprang from. That picture hangs above my desk as I write these words.

On my return to Rome I got a lot of fun out of turning up in uniform at places where I had not been known as a British officer. One of the funniest occasions was when I went into the Barber's shop in the Piazza Fiume where I had had my hair cut for the whole of the six months I was in Rome. As a British Officer I was given a flourishing welcome by the barber, who did not recognise me as I walked in in uniform, but when I took off my cap and he looked down at my thinning pate he recognised that at once. I was looking at his face in the mirror and the expression on it, when it dawned on him that he had been cutting a British officer's hair for the last six months, was truly comical and I seem to remember that I got a free hair-cut that day.

You would be forgiven for thinking that I was just showing off and I am sure that was partly what I wanted to do. But you must remember that I had been suspected of being a stool pigeon in some circles and I really did want to clean up my reputation in Rome once and for all. I did a broadcast on the Italian Radio. I had told the good people who had sheltered us on our way through the mountains that I would send them a 'Messagio Speciale' when I had reached our forces and that the message would be 'Meriela sta bene' (Meriel is well). Meriel was my daughter, whom I had never seen and whose photograph was shown to all our kind hosts until I lost it when I was arrested in Florence.

I wanted to thank those brave people who had sheltered us and fed us on our journey, I wanted to tell them that their efforts had been successful in my case and in many other cases, and encourage them to go on assisting prisoners still at large in the north. I wrote the script of the broadcast in Italian and it was then edited and 'improved' by the Italian Radio people and I found that when I had to deliver it I had to wrap my tongue round subjunctives and flowery phrases, which were very different from the utility stuff which had stood me in such good stead from day to day during the ten months I was on the run.

I particularly wanted to regain touch with the many A's and D's whom I had been forced to drop for one reason or another. I was able to invite them to meals, to meet me at the Hotel Eden and I very much appreciated being able to see Anneliese Chiarizia once again. I managed to get a large box at the Theatre where Irving Berlin gave a big concert in Rome for the troops and one of my Italian guests burst into many of the songs – he could not restrain himself. But he sang very well indeed and was roundly applauded.

I wanted to buy presents for my friends in Rome as mementos of the stormy days we had been through. To Lodzi I gave my Minox camera, which I had suitably engraved. With it we had managed to get documents photographed by Daniele. It was about the size of a small cigarette lighter. After shopping for presents in the Via Condotti (the Bond Street of Rome) and whilst delivering a very nice amber box to one of my Roman hostesses I came downstairs to find my little Fiat Topolino car sitting on its bottom in the gutter – some chaps had walked off with all four wheels! So it was back to the trams and buses and shanks' pony for me!

One of the first things that I did upon the arrival of the Allies in Rome was to send a telegram to my wife and mother to let them know that I was still alive, had reached the right side of the lines at last and ought soon to be on my way home. This message was sent via the Army Post Office people and, I expect because there must have been thousands of telegrams waiting to utilise the broken down, worn out or demolished Italian facilities, it never arrived, which was surprising when you think of the hundreds of messages I managed to send to the VIII Army before they arrived in Rome.

Even after the arrival of the Allies in Rome some funny things still happened to me. One day whilst out with Anneliese I saw two private soldiers of my own Regiment, wearing the uniform, equipment and cap badge that I had worn at Catterick Camp, when one night in 1939 our 1st Bn had marched down the hill to Richmond Station and to war. Furthermore they were wearing the same 5th Infantry Division flash on the sleeve of their jackets, the Francolin, because our Divisional Commander then was Major General Franklin. Perhaps the Battalion was in Rome or stationed nearby and I might be able to visit it, meet some old friends or, even better still, join it.

I went over to them, told them who I was and introduced them to Anneliese and starting talking about the Battalion. I asked if they were anywhere near Rome, when I saw with horror and dismay a dark look of suspicion cross their faces and I was seized and arrested.

''im and 'is German tart.'
And we were frogmarched off to the Military Police and cast into durance vile.

I suppose it was silly of me but I couldn't resist going over and having a chat with the first two soldiers of my old Battalion that I had seen since 1940. However I was quite used to being arrested in Rome and I had had some practice in getting Daniele out of clink since the arrival of the Allies, so it wasn't long before I was able to establish my identity and clear myself and with the help of Colonel Hill-Dillon, I was soon at large again once more. But I never found out where our 1st Bn was stationed.

My work in Rome was over. I was not well and I expect that Colonel Hill-Dillon thought that I ought to be sent home. That suited my book and so it was that I was flown to Algiers and from there to Rabat in a C47 Dakota – those Jeeps of the air of which the US Army seemed to have thousands. I had to hang around at Rabat for a while waiting for an RAF York aircraft to fly me back to England. It was a busy airport, most of the planes being American and ferrying men and equipment to and from America. The occasional heavily laden York would set off down the long runway towards the sunset and finally, when seemingly about to run out of runway and into the Atlantic, it would creep off the land more or less at the horizon. I remember an American officer who was watching this performance saying to me:

'Thank Gaad the earth is round.'

I think the War Office wanted to ask me some questions, so I was given a high priority and didn't have to wait too long. Soon it was my turn to climb into a York, set off down that runway and over the Atlantic and we flew all night I imagine well out to sea without any excitement.

The next morning looking out of the window I saw we were over the Bristol Channel and I could see Weston-super-Mare from where our 4th Battalion had set out for Egypt in 1941. We must have crossed the coast at Burnham-on-Sea and followed the broad green valley of the River Brue to Glastonbury and finally landed at an RAF airfield near Swindon. No sooner had the aircraft come to a halt than a thick white summer mist arose and enveloped us and they had to send a Jeep out to find us and guide us back to the airfield buildings.

After breakfast I managed to get a Rail Warrant to London and, as nobody seemed to be doing anything about getting me on my way, I hitched a lift in to Swindon, borrowed tuppence and rang up my mother at Lechlade who said:

'Wait a minute – don't dash off. I'll just pick some strawberries in the garden and come up to London with you.'

On the train I had news of my wife who was at the seaside at Rhosneigr in Anglesey and of my sister and the family. On arrival at Paddington we went to a hotel in South Kensington and I did a lot of telephoning.

After some sessions with the War Office and having got hold of some clothes and some money, I set off on the Holyhead train and there on the platform at Rhosneigr was my wife, Eileen, but she was practically invisible. She was standing facing the train as it came in and when I looked out she was standing sideways on in front of the station fence posts and was so thin she didn't show up against them.

I was then introduced to my 3½ year old daughter Meriel who was, I think, rather disappointed at meeting this odd-looking strange man who had now come between her and her Mummy. Indeed sitting on my knee at home a few days later and still trying to get acquainted she pointed to a photograph of me on the wall and said:

'My Daddy.'